RASPBERRY PI

FOR

BEGINNERS

TIPS AND TRICKS TO LEARN
RASPBERRY PI PROGRAMMING

Benjamin Wilson

TABLE OF CONTENTS

Chapter 1

Basics of Raspberry Pi

Introduction to Raspberry Pi

Raspberry Pi is a powerful device, an independent computer, and is sold at a highly competitive and affordable price. Raspberry Pi will support you in playing games, browsing the internet, learning to program, or creating your own physical devices. In this guide you will find step by step instructions for performing all these activities.

Raspberry Pi is a one-point computer; therefore, it is built on one single PCB. It will work like a computer, laptop, or smartphone. It is very small in size, like a credit card, and is powerful enough to compete with other similar devices. It can perform high functionality tasks like a computer does, but maybe not that much quicker.

The Raspberry Pi boards are used worldwide in offices, classrooms, data centers, homes, self-control boats, and small factories.

The first model released for the Raspberry Pi was model B. After that, there was no stopping it and many other models have been released to provide specific features or specifications for different use cases. For example, the Zero family of Raspberry Pi, which is a micro version of the complete Raspberry Pi, has dropped certain features such as wired network port and multiple USB options to have a small layout. This is particularly useful for those who need fewer power loads.

There is one thing common in all the Raspberry Pi models. They are compatible with each other, which means the programming software for a particular model will also run on any Raspberry Pi model. It works vice versa also;, you can have the latest operating system and then run it on the old prototype model. It will be a bit slow, but still, it will surely run. So that's the power of Raspberry Pi.

In this book, you will be focusing on the latest Raspberry Pi Model B+, which is also the most powerful version launched to date. Whatever you will learn here will also apply to other models. Thus you don't need to worry if you are working on a different model.

The Basics of Raspberry Pi

A computer hides all its working inside a case, but all components of Raspberry Pi can be seen, such as ports, wires, features, etc. If you prefer, you can buy a case from the market to have extra protection. This will help you to understand how exactly the parts of computer work. It will be interesting to learn how the peripherals work when connected with the PCB.

Pi 3 Model B+

At first look, it may seem like there are plenty of things packed into a very small board, yet it is very easy to understand Raspberry Pi. The best way to understand is to start with its components and the internal processes that make the device work.

The Basic Components of Raspberry Pi

The Pi, similar to other computers, consists of over a dozen components. Every part plays its specific role in making it work. The most important parts are located on the top of the board. This important part is protected by a metal cap named SOC. If you remove the metal cover, you will find a silicon chip, well known as an integrated circuit. This chip carries the majority parts of Raspberry Pi's structure. The parts it carries include the CPU, also known as the central processing unit, and the GPU, which deals with graphics and visual aspects of Raspberry Pi.

Figure 1: Raspberry Pi Board

RAM and SD Card

A brain without sufficient memory is of no use. In the base of the Raspberry Pi, one can see a small plastic chip, which is known as Pi's RAM or "random access memory." Whatever you do on your computer is controlled by the RAM. However, when you save your work, it goes to a micro SD card. The RAM forms the volatile memory of Raspberry Pi while the SD card forms its non-volatile memory. Things stored in RAM are short-lived; therefore, when you turn off your computer, it loses all its memory. On the other hand, the SD card will store things forever.

Radio

After turning the board sidewise of Raspberry Pi, you will find its radio covers in the metal lid on the upper side of it. The function of the radio is to enable Raspberry Pi to communicate with other devices without a wire. This radio can be divided into two types; the first type of radio named Wi-Fi radio is used to connect Raspberry Pi with other computer devices. The 2nd type of radio is Bluetooth radio, which is used to connect with nearby devices to share and receive data.

USB Controller and PMIC

The next component of a Raspberry Pi computer is a network and USB controller. It is located on the bottom side of the board. This component controls the Ethernet port and 4 USB ports. On the upper side of this USB controller is located PMIC, also known as "power management integrated circuit." Its function is to convert the power received from the USB port into the power required by the Pi to function.

The Types of Ports Used in Raspberry Pi

There is more than one type of port used in Raspberry Pi. The first and most prominent type is USB port that is normally four in number. These USBs are also known as USB 2.0 ports because they consist of 2nd version of USB (universal standard bus). These USB ports are useful for all types of USB compatible devices, including flash devices, mice, keyboards, etc. When you look towards the left side of these ports, you'll find the Ethernet port, which is used to connect Raspberry Pi with a wired computer network. If you look at this Ethernet port, you can see two status LEDs which convey the message if you are connected to a working network or not.

Headphone Jack

On the upper side of the Ethernet port, you can find the 3.5 mm headphone jack used for audiovisual. It can be used for an extra function, such as communicating audio signals to TVs and projectors etc. On the upper side of this AV jack is a camera connecter connected with pulled up plastic flap. This connecter is also called *Camera Serial Interface.* The function of this connecter is to allow you to use the Raspberry Pi camera module.

HDMI Port

On the left-hand edge of the same board is located the HDMI port. This port's function is to carry both audio and video signals of very high quality. This type of connector is mostly used in game consoles and TVs. This port is used to connect your Raspberry Pi to a display device. The display device can be a computer monitor, a projector, or a TV.

USB Power Port

On the upper side of the HDMI port is located micro USB power port. This port is used to connect your Raspberry Pi to an external power source. This micro USB port can be found on all types of smartphones and other portable devices, including tablets. Though you can use any standard charger to power the Raspberry Pi, for example, a tablet or smartphone charger, it is recommended that you use the original Raspberry Pi power supply.

Display Serial Interface

On the very top of the board is another connector that looks like a camera connector. It is a display connector, also known as Display Serial Interface. This port is specially designed to use for the touch display of Raspberry Pi.

GPIO Header

Now come towards the right-hand side of the board. Here one can easily locate a total of 40 pins made up of metal. These pins are separated into two parts of 20 pins each. These pins are called GPIO headers, also known as general-purpose input and output header. This GPIO header work as the special feature of Raspberry Pi as it accommodates additional hardware. Few examples of this hardware include LED's buttons, joysticks, temperature sensors, pulse rate sensors and monitors, and much more hardware.

On the same right-hand side, below this GPIO header is located 2nd header. This header is much smaller compared to the GPIO header and consists of 4 pins compared to whopping 40 pins in GPIO header. This small header is used to communicate with POE Hat, also known as Power over Ethernet HAT. This is an extra option of power supply to Raspberry Pi through a network connection, in case the main power source micro USB socket is not available or working.

Micro SD Card Connector

Last but not the least, there is one more port on the Raspberry Pi. This port is not present on the top; instead, you need to turn the board over to see the micro SD card connector port on the opposite side of the display connector of the board. This port is specified for the SD card or Raspberry Pi's storage. In this card, your saved files will be stored, your installed software's and the Raspberry Pi's running system are also stored in the micro SD card.

The Peripherals of Raspberry Pi

A Raspberry Pi can't work alone, much like a desktop computer cannot work without peripherals. To work properly and meaningfully, the Raspberry Pi system needs extra components. For example, a micro SD card for storage, a monitor for display purposes, and a keyboard to instruct the Raspberry Pi about what you want it to do are peripherals. Similarly, the power supply of 5 volts and 2.5 amps is also peripheral. Without these peripherals, a Raspberry Pi system can't function properly. These are just a few examples of peripherals; there are many more depending on the function you want from your Raspberry Pi.

Other official accessories produced or provided by the Raspberry Pi foundation are as follows: A camera module, a touch display related to Raspberry Pi, which used to provide video display and innovative touchscreen display after connecting with the display port of the system. Other official accessories include Raspberry Pi case, which is useful in protecting the Pi while keeping the access to necessary ports open, and a Sense HAT, which is a very innovative multifunctional addition to existing accessories.

Besides these official accessories, there are plenty of third party accessories available. These third-party accessories include useful kits to reshape your Raspberry Pi into a tablet and a laptop depending on your requirements. Other kits are also available that enable the Raspberry Pi to understand your spoken language, and a more advanced system will respond to your speech as well.

Chapter 2

Get Started with Raspberry Pi

Here we will explore the important things you require for your Raspberry Pi and how you can link them all to make it work and operate.

The Raspberry Pi has indeed been organized to be as prompt and convenient to set up and use as feasible. Still, it depends on multiple operational elements, called peripherals, just like every other computer. While it is indeed convenient to look at the Raspberry Pi's bare circuit board, it is very different from the enclosed, shuttered-off computers that you might be used to. You may feel worried that it will be complex to use, but that is not the case. With the Raspberry Pi, you can also be fully operational in less than 10 minutes merely by following the instructions in this chapter.

Raspberry Pi 3 Model B+ Requirements

If you already have the Raspberry Pi Starter Kit, you have almost all you need to get started. All you need is a desktop computer or HDMI-connected TV – the same sort of cable used mostly by set-top boxes, Blu-ray players, and gaming systems – so you could see what the Raspberry Pi does. If you would not have the Raspberry Pi Starter Kit, you will require, in order having access to the Raspberry Pi 3 Model B+:

Standard USB Supply – a 2.5 Amp (2.5A) or 12.5 watts (12.5W) power connection and a micro USB adapter. The Authorized

Raspberry Pi power source is the preferred option since it can deal with the Raspberry Pi's fast-changing electricity needs.

NOOBS Micro SD Card – The micro SD card functions as long term storage of Raspberry Pi. The documents you make and the software you download, including the web browser itself, are saved in the micro SD card. You'll begin with an 8 GB card. However, a 16 GB one provides more space to develop. Use of a pre-loaded NOOBS card, the new out-of-box software, protects you sometimes; otherwise, you can also decide to deploy NOOBS on an empty micro SD card.

USB Keypad and Mouse - The Raspberry Pi can be operated by the mouse and keyboard. Nearly all wired or wireless keyboards and mice, using a USB adapter, would function with the Raspberry Pi. Although a few bright lights-style 'gaming' keyboards can consume too much energy to use reliably.

HDMI Cable – The HDMI cable delivers audio and images to your TV or monitor from the Raspberry Pi. Hence it is not essential to waste much cash on an HDMI cable. You can purchase Display Port, VGA adapters, or HDMI to DVI-D when you're using a computer screen without an HDMI plug. If you'd like to attach your Raspberry Pi to an old TV that uses a SCART Plug or composite clip, choose an audio/video cable with a 3.5 mm tip-ring-sleeve (TRRS).

Even without a case, the Raspberry Pi would be secure to use, given that you do not put it on a metal that might conduct current and end up causing a small explosion. Nevertheless, an additional cover will give extra security; the Starter Kit includes the Original Raspberry Pi Cover, whereas covers from third parties are accessible from all of the great online stores.

You'll also require a network cable if you're using the Raspberry Pi on a wired connection instead of a wireless (Wi-Fi) connection. That must be attached to the switch or adapter of your network at one point. If you are willing to utilize the built-in wireless radio from the Raspberry Pi, you will not require a wire; but, you still need to remember your wireless network's name and key or password.

Organizing the Equipment

Start by unwrapping your Raspberry Pi out of its case. The Raspberry Pi is a strong piece of equipment. However, that doesn't mean it's invulnerable. Be careful when you handle it; lift it by the corners only and be very careful around the pins. If these pins have become bent, it would then, at greatest, make it complicated to use add-on boards as well as other extra hardware. At worst, it could even end up causing a small explosion that harms the Raspberry Pi. If you haven't yet done so, check out Chapter 1 for info about specifically where the ports are, including what they involve doing.

Putting the Case Together

If you download your Pi, that should be your first move. If you are utilizing the authorized Raspberry Pi Case, start by dividing it into five separate items: the red base, two white sides, the red upper, and the white lid.

Figure 2: Raspberry Pi Case

Consider taking the core and keep it so that the elevated side is to the left and the bottom side to the right. Carrying the Pi through its USB and Ethernet terminals, with the GPIO header to the highest point, plug the left side into the case at an angular position. Then softly lessen the right side downwards so that it lays smooth.

Grab the two white side parts and locate the one with the power connection cut-outs, the HDMI port and the 3.5 mm AV socket. Match it along with the Raspberry Pi terminals, and drive it home softly unless you detect a sound.

Grab the strong white side portion and press it into the case section of the GPIO connector. Grab the upper part of red plastic and put the two clips on the left, just above the micro SD card slot, in the pairing gaps on the left of the core. Force the right side (over the USB ports) down till you lis10 to tap when they are in position.

Eventually, grab the white lid and keep it so that the Raspberry Pi symbol is to your right as well as the tiny clips held on its lower part are set up with the pit at the highest point of the case, then move it carefully down until you notice a tap. Your case is in full construction already.

Linking the Micro SD Card

Flip the Raspberry Pi over and drag the card into the micro SD socket with the tag direction away from the Pi to download the micro SD card, which is also the Raspberry Pi's memory. It will only go in one direction, and therefore should move home without excessive pressure.

The micro SD card moves into the adapter and then closes without even a single tap. In the coming years, if you'd like to delete it once again, simply take the end of the card and slowly bring it out. Unless you're using an older Raspberry Pi system, first, you'll have to give the card a slight nod to activate it; with a Raspberry Pi 3 or modern, that's not essential.

Linking a Mouse and a Keyboard

Plug the USB on the keyboard to one of Raspberry Pi's four USB ports. When connecting the keyboard, just apply the same method when connecting the mouse. The keyboard and mouse USB adapters will slip home despite excessive pressure; if you have to push the connector in, something went incorrect. Verify that the USB connector is the correct way up!

The keyboard and mouse serve as the primary tool of saying the Raspberry Pi how to do it; they are classified as input devices in programming, in comparison to the monitor that is an output device.

Joining a Display

Get the HDMI cable and attach one side to your Raspberry Pi and the other side to your monitor. If your device does have more than one HDMI port, search for a port number beside the adapter itself; to view the Pi display, you'll have to shift the TV to such input. If you are unable to see a port number, don't stress: you can shift in turn through every input until you figure the Pi.

TV Network

If your television or computer has no HDMI plug, it shouldn't mean you can't use the Raspberry Pi. Connector cables, accessible from every other electronics storage unit, permit you to transform the Raspberry Pi VGA, Display Port, or HDMI port to DVI-D to be used with older computer screens. They are connected directly to the Pi HDMI port, then an appropriate cable for connecting the connector cable to the monitor. You can buy 3.5 mm tip-ring-sleeve (TRRS) connector cables and composite-to-SCART adapters that mostly attach to the 3.5 mm AV jack unless your TV has just a composite visual or SCART input.

Attaching an Ethernet Cable (non-mandatory)

A network cable – known as an Ethernet cable – is required to attach your Raspberry Pi to a wireless connection and move it to the Pi Ethernet port, with the plastic clipping pointing down until you notice a tap. If you want to detach the cable, simply pull the plastic clip in towards the socket and slide the cable carefully away again. In the very same manner, you should attach the other side of your network cable with any free port on the network hub, switch, or modem.

Link an Electric Power Supply

Linking the Raspberry Pi to a power source is the last move in the device configuration process, but it is one you must only do when you're ready to build its operating system. The Raspberry Pi has no power button and will switch on as long as it's attached to a live power source. After this, attach the micro USB end of the electric power cable to the Raspberry Pi micro USB power adapter. It will only go in one direction, with the wide portion of the connector pointing down, and will carefully slip around.

Power Distribution

If you're running the Original Raspberry Pi power source, you'll see this one arrives with various handheld connectors appropriate for different country sockets. Choose the one that matches the plug type of your country, and move it onto the power distribution body till you notice a sound. Afterward, link the power source to a plug on the main supply and turn the plug on; the Raspberry Pi begins to run instantly.

Big congrats: You've built Raspberry Pi!

Establishing the Software Program

Before you could even start using the Raspberry Pi, you'll have to build its programming – particularly its software platform, the software that governs what the Pi could do. NOOBS, the New Out-Of-Box Software, is created to make this simple and easy, letting you pick spontaneously from installing multiple software. Effectively yet, you could do all that in just a few mouse clicks. You can see a display with the Raspberry Pi icon on it and a tiny status window at the top-left whenever the Pi is first turned on or loaded with a new version of NOOBS over its micro SD card. After a quick break, you would see the display.

No Display?

If you cannot view the Raspberry Pi on your screen, please check that the right input is being utilized. If your Television or monitor contains more than one HDMI input, select the 'Source' or 'Out' button to cycle across each in order until the NOOBS list appears.

Figure 3: Installation

This is indeed the NOOBS menu, a program that allows you to select the web browser you want to operate on your Pi. Many computer systems are included as standard with NOOBS: Raspbian, an edition of the Debian Linux operating system designed exclusively to the Raspberry Pi, and others, as shown in the above image. You may even install and update other software systems if the Pi is linked to the internet - either by a wired connection or use the 'Wi-Fi network (w)' option on the upper icon bar.

Now use the cursor to insert a cross in the window to the left of Raspbian Full to start running software. Move the pointer to the white box, and tap once with the left mouse button. When you do this, you will see that the 'Install (i)' menu figure is not greyed-out anymore; this way, you will come to know that your software is ready for deployment.

Figure 4: Installation Progress

Press the 'Install (i)' icon once from the left mouse click, and you will get an alert telling you that any documents presently saved on the micro SD card will be overwrit10 by deploying the software - not counting NOOBS on its own, which remains unchanged. Click 'Yes,' and deployment starts.

Based on the frequency of your micro SD card, the configuration process could take from 10 to 30 minutes. As the software is mounted, progression is displayed in a bar at the base of the screen. In Chapter 3, you will learn more about using your Raspberry Pi and the system software.

Important Tips and Tricks while Installing Raspberry Pi

It is necessary not to disrupt the deployment, as it has a strong probability of destroying the program, a mechanism known as data corruption. Do not detach the micro SD card or disconnect the power cable when the software is operational. Instead, disconnect the Pi from its power source if there is something that prevents the deployment, after which press and hold the SHIFT key on the keyboard while connecting the Raspberry Pi back to its power source to reset the NOOBS menu. This is recognized as recovery mode and seems to be a wonderful way to rebuild a Pi whose work order software has been corrupted once more. This also helps you to join the NOOBS menu after an update, to reformat or upgrade the operating system.

A window would then be displayed with an 'OK' tab just after setup is finished; select this and the Pi will reboot into its freshly appointed software. You will see a lot of text fast-forwarding up the window. These are the boot notifications, and it can take a couple of minutes for the first time you boot through Raspbian. It changes itself to make proper use of the space available on your micro SD. The next time you do it, it will be faster.

After that, just before the Raspbian computer and configuration browser appears, you'll view a screen only with the Raspberry Pi sticker on it for a moment. You are now completely downloaded and prepared to customize your web browser, which you will know and will understand in Chapter 3, using your Raspberry Pi

Chapter 3

How to Use your Raspberry Pi

Raspberry Pi is a versatile system that can run various types of software. It can handle even operating systems that are required to run a computer. The most useful and popular of these operating systems is none other than the official operating system of Raspberry Pi, i.e., the Raspbian. Dependent on the Debian Linux, Raspbian is specifically designed for the Raspberry Pi system. It is equipped with a wide variety of pre-installed and ready-made applications.

If you are only familiar with the Apple macOS or Microsoft Windows, there is nothing to worry about Raspbian as it comes with almost the same functions and display features, including similar windows, menus, icons, and pointer principles.

Setting up Raspberry Pi for your First Use

The Greeting Wizard

If you are running the Raspbian for the first time, you will be greeted with a welcome wizard. This very useful tool will help you make some important setting changes, also known as the configuration. If you are not interested in the welcome wizard, you have the option to cancel it, but keep in mind that you can't access some important features of Raspberry Pi, for example, wireless network. To access these basic features, answer the first set of simple questions in the welcome wizard.

Setting Up the Raspberry Pi Password

You can begin a welcome wizard tour by clicking on the Next button. The next step is to choose your country, language, and time zone of your country. After putting this information, click the next button. On the next screen, you need to choose a password. Interestingly, most of the users have the password 'raspberry.' But having a password which is underuse of so many Raspberry Pi users will put you on a security risk if you choose the same password. Therefore, reset the existing password and choose a new one that is only known to you. After choosing an appropriate password, click 'next'.

Setting Up the Wi-Fi Password

On the next screen, you need to set up another password, this time for the Wi-Fi. To set up the password, select your Wi-Fi network from the given list of networks and after selecting click 'next'. As your wireless network is secure, you need to put its password in the given box. If you don't wish to connect with the wireless network at this time, skip the step by clicking on the skip button.

Installing the Updates for Raspbian

The next screen is all about Raspbian updates and their installation. Raspbian provides regular updates to fix the system glitches, introduce new features, and boost the performance. If you are interested in installing these updates, click 'next.' If you are not interested in these updates, click on 'skip.'

Rebooting

The last screen of the greeting wizard is all about rebooting the Raspberry Pi. Certain changes are valid only if you reboot or restart the Raspberry Pi. Click on the reboot option when it appears, and Raspberry Pi will restart automatically. After starting again, the welcome wizard will not appear again; this means your Raspberry Pi is finally ready to use.

Desktop Navigation

In the majority of the Raspberry Pi boards, the 'Raspbian with the Raspberry Pi Desktop' version is used. This version is named after its principal graphical user interface. The large portion of this desktop is covered with a wallpaper picture. On the top left side of this wallpaper, the installed programs you use will appear. There is a taskbar on the upper side of the desktop; the function of this taskbar is to assist you in loading every program. The loaded programs are shown in the taskbar as tasks.

On the right side of the menu bar, a system tray is located. On the right side of this tray is an eject symbol. When you click on the eject symbol, a list of removable storage will appear. The removal storage includes any connected USB memory. This eject function also allows us to remove the removal storages safely.

Next to this eject option is a clock. If you want to check the calendar, click on this clock. Near this clock and calendar lies a box attached with a scrolling line graph that contains a number on it. This box is a CPU monitor that informs you how easy or load-free your computer is working right now. If you see a low number, for example, 0 or 5%, this means your computer is working very little. If you see a higher number, say 90 0r 100%, your Raspberry Pi is working hard.

Next to this box is the speaker symbol. If you want to adjust music volume, click on it, and use your mouse to adjust Pi's volume according to requirement. Next to this speaker symbol, the network icon is present. When you are connected to your home Wi-Fi or any other network, its signal strength is shown here. In the case of a Wi-Fi network, you'll see a series of bars while, in case of a wired network, two arrows will appear. Click on this network icon to see how many networks are currently available; you can change your network here.

Very next to the network icon reside the Bluetooth icon. Click on this icon to connect with nearby available Bluetooth devices. These icons are on the right side of the icon; let's check what is present on the left side of the Desktop. A menu bar is located on the left side of the desktop. In this menu bar, the launcher is located; in the launcher, all the installed programs are present, including the Raspbian. A few of these programs are present as shortcuts, while other programs are located in the menu. You can access these programs by clicking on the Raspberry icon present on the extreme left side.

All programs present in the launcher are divided into different categories. For example, in the programming category, only those software are present that help in creating your programs. In the game category, all installed games are available.

Chromium Web Browser

To learn using your Raspberry Pi, open the Chromium web browser. In the browser, you can see the Raspberry icon located on the top side of the menu. Using your mouse pointer, choose the internet category and command the Chromium web browser to open it.

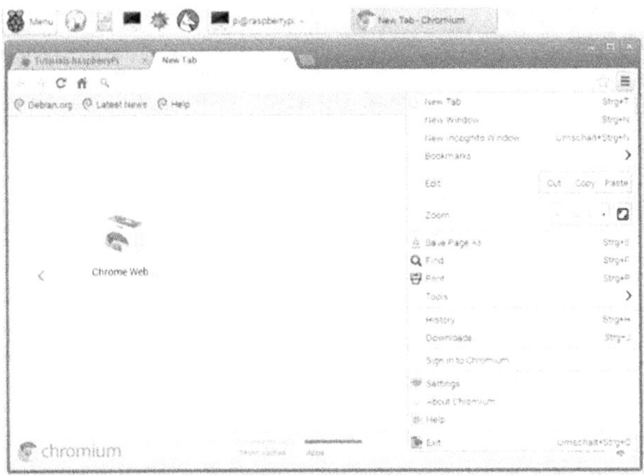

Figure 5: Chromium Web Browser

This browser is very similar to the Google Chrome browser, therefore if you are currently using the Google Chrome browser, using Chromium Browser will not be a difficult task. The Chromium browser allows you to search websites, download and play video games, and talk with other people from all over the world at one click. When you decide to use the Chromium browser, do it by maximizing its window so that it can cover most of the Raspberry Pi screen. There are up to three icons located on the upper side of the browser's window title bar, click on the middle icon which looks like a box. This button's function is to maximize the window to fill the screen. On the left side of this button, minimize option is located, which is used to hire a window. On the right side of the maximize button, the close option is present, which used to close the window.

To open the Raspberry Pi website on the browser, click on the address bar located on the top side of the browser window. After clicking on the address bar, type or paste the address www.raspberrypi.org and click on the Enter key. Besides typing the whole address, you can type keywords like 'Raspberry Pi' and 'Educational Computing' etc.

When you access the Chromium for the first time, it opens several tabs on the top of the window. In order to switch to another tab, just click on it. If you want to close a particular tab without closing the main Chromium window, click on the cross present on that tab. To open multiple websites, you need to open more tabs. In order to open new tabs, click on the tab button on the right side of the last tab. There is a 2nd option to create a new tab, just click CTRL key present on the bottom side of the keyboard along with the T key. When you have finished searching stuff on the Chromium browser, press the close button present on the top right side of the window.

File Manager

All types of saved files, including created videos, songs, programs, MS office files, and all types of other files and programs, go to only one place named 'Home Directory.' To access the home directory, click the Raspberry Pi icon to see open the menu. Through the mouse, select the Accessories option and press the File Manager to open it.

The File Manager function is to allow you to search your required files and folders, also named as the 'directories.' The same is valid for the Raspberry Pi's micro SD card and other removable memory devices. Similar to the USB drives, you connect with the Raspberry Pi's specific ports. When you open it for the first time, it moves to the home directory automatically. In here, you can see numerous other folders named as subdirectories. These subdirectories folders are also present in categories. Some of the subdirectories are given below:

Desktop

When you open your Raspbian, this is the first folder you will see. Saving any file here means, the file will appear on the desktop of the Raspberry Pi. It is more convenient to open a file from the desktop.

Documents and Downloads

The document subdirectory holds most of your created files, starting from short stories to manuals. When you download a file using the built-in browser, Chromium, or any other browser, it will go to the Download folder.

Music, Pictures, and Videos

In the music folder, all types of download or created music will be stored. On the other hand, the picture folder contains only pictures. It is also known as image files while the Video folder, as the name depicts, is specific for saving videos.

Public

There are some files you will like to keep private, don't save those files here. If you want some files to keep open for the public, save here, these files will always be available for other Raspberry Pi users.

The File Manager is divide into two panes; the left pane is all about the directories, and the right pane is reserved for the files and subdirectories of that directory you chose on the left pane. Whenever you put a removable storage device into the USB port, a new window will appear with a message to open this storage device in the file manager. If you like to open it and see its directories and files, click on the OK option.

Copying the File to Raspberry Pi's MicroSD Card

Copying the file from any removable device to Raspberry Pi's microSD card and vice versa is easier than you think. Open the home directory and removable device separately on the file manager. Now, move the mouse pointer to the selected file for copy, click on the file and drag it to the 2nd window. Release the mouse after the file has reached the 2nd window. This method of copying is called 'dragging and dropping.'

There is another option available to copy the file. Click only once on the file you want to copy, click on the edit menu, you will see multiple options, click on the Copy option. After this, click on the other window option, choose the Edit menu, and finally click on the Paste option to paste the file. The move option is also available to send the file to the target location, but the only difference is it deletes the file from its original location.

If you don't have a mouse, you can use the shortcut keys from the keyboard to perform the above-given operations. Use CTRL+C to copy and CTRL+X to cut; to paste, click CTRL+V. After learning and performing these operations, close the File Manager via clicking the close option at the top left corner of the window. If you want to eject a removable disk, remove it by clicking the eject button present on the top right side of the screen.

The Productivity Suite

Besides the above-given functions, Raspberry Pi can perform a series of other functions. Go to the Raspberry menu icon, open the Office, here you will find the LibreOffice writer, click on it. After clicking on it, the word processor portion of LibreOffice will open. LibreOffice is a well-known productivity suite, used to make documents of different types. It is very similar to MS Office and Google Docs. If you have experience of working on any of this software, you can use LibreOffice easily.

The function of a word processor, including LibreOffice, is not only to write documents conveniently but also to format them innovatively. For example, you can change the font size, color, and styles, insert pictures, charts, and similar con10t. Word processor also used to detect and correct mistakes, highlight the important con10t, check grammar mistakes, and many more.

You can test the LibreOffice productivity suite by writing a paragraph about the Raspberry Pi. Check the icons given on the top to learn what they do and implement all the changes in fonts you can make using all the features of the office. If you are not sure about each icon, take your mouse pointer near the icon, a tooltip will pop up to guide you what the pointed icon does. To save the work you have done so far, go to the File menu and click on the Save option, provide a name to save that work.

The writing part of the LibreOffice is just a small part of the LibreOffice productivity suite. The other parts of the productivity suite are as follows:

LibreOffice Base

This is a database tool for storing information, check it quickly, and analyze it in a fast manner.

LibreOffice Calc

It is a spreadsheet tool for managing numbers well, create charts, as well as the graphs.

LibreOffice Draw

It is an illustration program used for creating and editing pictures and diagrams.

LibreOffice Impress

It is a presentation program, used to create slides and run slideshows.

LibreOffice Math

It is a formula editor used to format mathematical formulas.

If you like the LibreOffice on Raspberry Pi and want to run it on other systems, for example, Microsoft Windows, Apple macOS, and Linux computer, fortunately, it can be used in these systems. For this purpose, you can download it free from libreoffice.org and install on these systems easily.

Useful Software Tool

By default, Raspbian is equipped with a wide variety of software and is workable with even more software. A wide range of compatible software chosen by the Raspberry Pi administration is provided in the recommended Software Tool section. If you like one or more software provided in this section, connect to the internet and download them. When your Raspberry Pi is connected with the internet connection, a list of compatible software appears in the preferences tool.

These recommended and compatible software are present in an arranged form, similar to software present in the Raspberry menu. Click on the category you like the most in pane located on the left side to check software in that category. You can see all the recommended software by clicking on all programs.

If a tick is present on software, this means it is already installed in your Raspberry Pi. It a tick is not there, and you want to download or install it, just click on the checkbox present near to it. You can install as many software as you like until the storage of the micro SD card is full. Uninstall unwanted software to create space for new software. You can uninstall any software by unticking the installed software. There is another tool named as Add/Remove Software tool to install/uninstall any software. It can be located in the Preferences category of the Raspbian menu.

Configuration Tool of Raspberry Pi

The last and final program of this chapter that one needs to learn in order to understand Raspbian software is the Raspberry Pi Configuration tool. This tool is very helpful in changing different settings in Raspbian. To access this tool, click on the Raspbian icon and go to the Preferences category. Here you will find the Raspberry Pi Configuration tool; click on it to load it.

The tool is divided into four important tabs, each one controlling some critical features of the Raspbian. The first tab is known as the system tab. The tab is mostly concerned with changing passwords, set a new hostname, and a wide range of other settings that need change, though most of the settings don't need any change.

The next tab is the Interfaces tab that brings the next type of settings. These settings need a change when you are setting up new hardware in your Raspberry Pi. An example of it can be the Camera Module. However, some changes are necessary to make like SSH that creates a secure shell required for you to log into the Raspberry Pi from any other system as well.

To access the third category of settings, click on the Performance tab. In this tab, Raspberry Pi 's performance-related functions are the main focus. In this tab, you can set the actual amount of memory Raspberry Pi's GPU can use. In the same tab, you'll find a process known as overclocking to manifold the performance of Raspberry Pi.

Fourth and the final tab is the Localization tab. This is mostly concerned with the location of your Raspberry Pi. Location plays an important role as it will decide the language of your Raspberry Pi. Change the location to select the language you want from your Raspberry Pi. Using the same tab, you can select a different time zone, vary the keyboard layout, and select the country for the WiFi network.

Shutting Down

After learning a different aspect of the Raspbian desktop, it's time to learn about other important aspects of it. The most important skill to learn is safely shutting down the Raspberry Pi. It is important to learn that Raspberry Pi keeps your data and files you are working on in volatile memory. This type of memory is not permanent and will vanish once you turn off your computer. To keep important files for longer duration in the system, you need to save them in the microSD card.

When you are working on these files when the Raspberry Pi is ON, there are plenty of other files and software open when the system is running. When the power source suddenly pulled off, can danger the survival of the operating system. It is observed that when the power source is turned off without properly shutting down the Raspberry Pi, it can make the operating system corrupt and may need to be reinstalled.

To avoid such a situation, save the opened files and make the system itself ready to turn off securely. This process is called as shutting down of the Raspberry Pi. To shut down the system, click on the Raspberry icon located on the top left side of the desktop; you will find the option of Shutdown. Select this option and Shutdown the computer/ Raspberry Pi.

There are other options available besides the shutdown, for example, Reboot and Logout. A reboot is very similar to the Shutdown where everything closes down but restarts again after a while. The logout option is useful only when you have multiple user accounts on Raspberry Pi. Clicking on this option results in the closing of all programs currently running, and the login screen will appear. You can choose another account by putting the user name and password..

Chapter 4

Tips and Tricks to Learn Scratch Programming in Raspberry Pi

Here we will study how to begin programming with Scratch, the block-dependent software platform.

Utilizing a Raspberry Pi is not only about using various software made by others. It's also about constructing your own software, depending on about anything your creativity can think up. If you have prior experience with designing your original software-a method recognized as coding or programming-or not, the Raspberry Pi is indeed a perfect tool for innovation and creativity.

Scratch, a graphic computer language established by the Massachusetts Institute of Technology (MIT), is crucial to the availability of coding on the Pi. Other conventional software requires you to compose text-based commands for the desktop to perform, in just the same manner as you would write down a cake baking recipe. By contrast, Scratch uses blocks to construct your system by a series of steps, pre-designed pieces of code concealed underneath parts of the color-coded puzzle.

Scratch is a fantastic introductory language for young and old aspiring coders; at the same time, do not be deceived by its pleasant looks. It's a strong and completely operational development tool that produces everything, including easy games and animations, to advanced immersive robotics programs.

Establishing Scratch 2 Interface

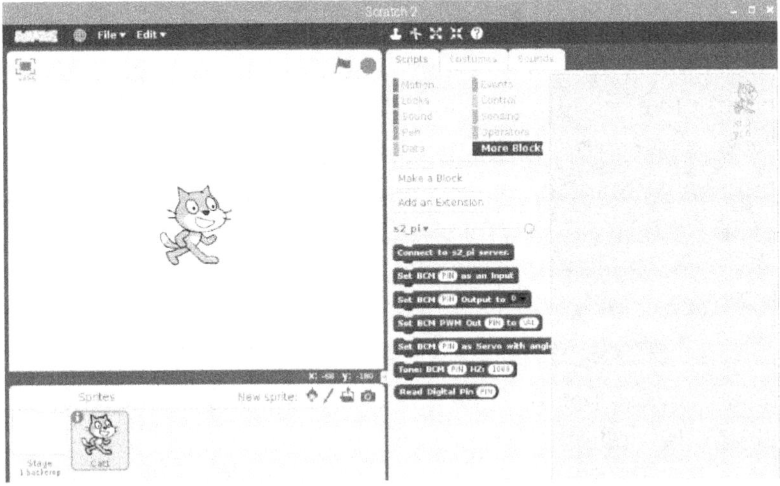

Figure 6: Scratch 2 Interface

Stage Area – Just like performers in a play, your sprites migrate around the frame.

Sprite – The Scratch system's figures or items that you command are identified as sprites and sit on the floor.

Stage Authorities – The stage can also be modified by using stage functions, like using your own images as templates.

Sprites Menu – This window segment will display here all sprites you have generated or mounted to Scratch.

Blocks Palette – The blocks palette that contains color-coded classes appears in all of the blocks accessible for your system.

Blocks – Pre-composed pieces of programming language, blocks enable you to step-by-step construct your system.

Scripts Field – The scripts area would be where the drag-and-drop frames from the blocks palette build your system.

SCRATCH Editions

Raspbian arrived with two editions of Scratch at the moment: the actual Scratch as well as the modified Scratch 2 each included in the Raspbian menu's coding portion. This page is composed for Scratch 2. Please ensure you do not accidentally launch the actual Scratch! Unfortunately, Scratch 2 will not be operating on the Pi Zero, Model A, A+, B, or B+.

Your First Scratch Software: Hey, World!

Scratch 2 starts like any other system on the Pi: to install the Raspbian menu, tap on the Raspberry symbol, start moving the pointer to the coding segment, and tap on Scratch 2. The Scratch 2 client interface would then install after just a couple of seconds.

Where you have to inform the machine what to do via composed commands in several programming languages, Scratch is unique. Begin by selecting the Looks section in the palette of blocks, located in the Scratch window core. This mentions the blocks, colored purple, under that particular group. Search the **"Say Hello!"** block, Press and keep the left mouse button on it and move it to the script region on the right side of the Scratch screen before you allow the mouse button to move.

Have a glance at the block shape you've pulled. It's got a pit at the upper end and a contrasting portion at the lower part. This tells you, like just a puzzle part, that the block needs something beyond it, and something underneath it. That anything above is a catalyst for this software. Tap on the Blocks palette Events tab, painted light brown, then press and move the block – identified as a hat block – to the script region when pressed. Place it so that the piece that pops out from the base attaches to the top hole of your **say Hello!** Block till a white overview is visible, and just let the mouse button move. You shouldn't have to be accurate; if it is close quite so, much like a puzzle segment, the block will flip into location. If it doesn't, then once again tap and drag on to change its location until it seems to.

Your system is now complete. Press on the green flag symbol at the upper end of the screen area to make it function, recognized as operating the software. If all went smoothly on board the cat sprite would welcome you with a happy 'Hello! '- Your program worked perfectly!

Name and backup your program before doing the next task. Select the file menu after this select Save Project. Enter a title and press Save.

Next Steps: Arranging

While there are two blocks in your software, it just has one true command: say 'Hello!' Each time you click on the flag, and now the system operates. You have to understand much more about arranging to do the later tasks. Computer systems are a sequence of commands at its easiest, much like a recipe. Every guideline in a natural sequence recognized as a linear sequence implements from the last.

Begin by pressing and moving the say Hello! Limit back to block palette from the scripts field. It erases the button, eliminates it from your software, and, when pressed, leaves only the control mark.

Tap on the Motion section in the blocks palette, after this press and move the 10 steps block movement so that it seals the scripts field under the block control. As the title indicates, this informs your sprite — the cat — to make a series of moves in the path it is on.

Insert more guidelines to build a series into your software. Tap on the color-coded pink sound palette, after which press and move the play audio meow until the block is completed, so it seals 10 steps block under the step. Continue: Select the Motion section and move another 10 steps block under your Audio block. However, this time tap the '10' to pick it and enter '-10' to construct a move -10 series block.

To operate the program, press on the green flag over the point. You can notice the cat shift to the right, produce a meow tone-please ensure you have headphones or speakers attached to lis10 to it and switch back to the start. Once more press on the flag, and now the cat reiterates its moves.

Congrats: you produced a pattern of commands that Scratch operates from beginning to end, one at a time. Although Scratch just executes one command at a time again from the menu and does so quite rapidly, attempt to delete the play audio meow before the block is completed by pressing and moving the bottom movement -10 steps block to remove it, add the play audio meow to its blocks palette, after this substitute it with the easier meow block play tone prior to actually moving your push -10 steps block down to the base of your program.

To operate the program again, press the green flag, but the cat model doesn't appear to move. The sprite is indeed relocating, but it is also shifting back so fast that it seems to be hanging still. That is because utilizing the play audio meow framework doesn't stay until the sound stops working until the final step. Since the Raspberry Pi 'thinks' very fast, the new command operates until you can actually notice the cat sprite moving. There's already a way to solve this, outside of using the play audio meow until the block is completed. Tap on the block palette control section, color-coded gold, after this select and move a pause block between the play audio meow block and the lower part movement -10 steps block.

Tap on the green flag to operate your program this last time, and you will find the cat sprite is expecting for a moment after shifting to the right prior to actually shifting back to the left once more. This is recognized as delay and is crucial to managing how much your command series will take to function.

Cycling the Loop

The series you produced so far just operates once. You press on the green flag, the transitions as well as meows of the cat sprite, and afterward, the system shuts down until you press the green flag once more. However, it doesn't have to quit, since Scratch contains a Control block form recognized as a loop.

Tap on the block palette control portion, color-coded gold, and search the forever block. Press and move this into the region of the scripts, and drop it underneath the block selected and the 10 steps block in front of the first step.

Note how even the C-shaped forever block in your series would eventually expand to cover the surrounding blocks. Press just on the green flag, and you'll immediately see what this forever block is really doing. Rather than operating your program once and for all, this should operate again and again – basically forever. This is recognized as an infinite loop in coding-truly, a loop that never finishes.

If you hear a little part of the audio of continual meowing, hit the red octagon besides the green flag just above stage field to end your project. Press and move the first 10 steps block to modify the loop form; drag it and the blocks below out of the forever block, after which, you lower them below the block when pressed. Tap and move the forever block to that same palette of blocks to erase it, after this tap and move the repetition 10 blocks underneath the block that is tapped to go around many blocks.

To operate your latest project, tap on the green flag. Initially, it would seem to perform the exact thing as your previous form: reiterating your guidance pattern again and again. This time, however, the chain will end after 10 repeats instead of running indefinitely. This is called a definite loop: you describe when this is going to end. Loops are essential tools, and several projects make ex10sive consumption of both definite and infinite loops – mainly games and detecting projects.

Variables and Conditional Statements

Before starting to program Scratch software in detail, the final principles to be grasped are strongly linked: variables and conditionals. As the title indicates, a variable is a quantity that can differ – that is, change – across time or under software control. There are two major features of a variable: its name, and the valuation it holds. There is no need for that value to just be a number at all: this can be figures, text, accurate-or-false, or entirely vacant – recognized as null.

Variables are very powerful if you use them wisely. Think about the stuff you need to monitor in a game: a character's fitness, the velocity of moving target, the existing standard of competition, and the ranking. These are all monitored as variables.

Initially, by tapping the Save Project, press the file button, and start saving your current plan. After that, select the file button and then the New to begin a fresh task. In the blocks palette, tap on the Data group, after this, the 'Make a Variable' button. Enter 'loops' as the label of the variable, then press the OK key to bring up a sequence of blocks throughout the palette of blocks.

Press on the scripts section and move the fixed loops to 0 levels. This informs your software to configure the 0-value variable. Then, tap on the palette's Looks section, and move the say Hello! for 2 seconds frame below your schedule loops to 0 blocks.

As you noticed earlier, the say Hello! Blocks allow the cat sprite to tell something that's programmed into them. However, you can utilize a variable rather than typing the text in the block directly. Scroll back on the data section in the palette of blocks, and then select and move the block of curved loops – identified as a reporter block and also observed at the top of the menu, with a checkbox beside it – over the term 'Hello!' inside your say Hello! For 2 seconds block. This introduces a unique, merged block: claim 2-sec cycles.

Press within the blocks palette on the Events section, afterward tap and move the block to the edge of the pattern of your block when pressed. Select the green flag outside the stage zone where you will notice the cat sprite reading '0' - the number you provided to the 'loops' variable.

Nevertheless, variables aren't immutable. Press on the data section in the Blocks Palette, then select and move the alter loops by 1 block downwards of your pattern. After that, press the Control section, then tap and move a recurrence 10-block and put it back so that it begins effectively below your 0-block schedule loops and folds across the unused blocks in your series.

Tap once more on the green flag. This moment, the cat report from 0 to 9 will be noticed on the top. This functions if the software either updates or modifies the variable itself: the software attaches one to that number in the 'loops' variable each time the process operates.

Note: Though the cycle you generated operates 10 times, the cat sprite adds up only up to nine times. This is since, for our variable, we begin with just worth of zero. There are 10 figures among zero and nine like zero and nine - and the system ends before the cat even mentions '10.' To modify this, you may correct the starting value of the variable to 1 rather than 0.

With a variable, you can perform much more than just configure it. Tap and move the say cycles for a period of 2 secs to separate it out of the replicate 10 block and put it under the replicate 10 block. To erase it, press and move the replicate 10 block towards the blocks palette, after that in place of it, put a replicate until block, ensuring that the block is attached to the downward of loops just for 2 secs block as well as adjoin the other two blocks in your pattern. Press on the Operators section there in Blocks palette, color-coded green, after this tap and move the diamond-shaped n = n block and put it on the contrasting diamond-shaped pit in the reiteration till block.

This block of the Operators allows you to relate two values along with variables. Tap the Data section in the block palette, move the reporter loop block in the initial vacant square in the n = n Operators block, after this tap the next vacant square, and write the '10' number.

Press on the green flag just above stage field, and you will discover that the system runs a certain manner it did previously: the cat sprite adds up from 0 to 9, and afterward, the system halts.

The above is because the repetition till block operates pretty much the same way as the repeat 10 blocks, but instead of adding up the value of loops by itself, the worth of the 'loops' variable is matched to the value you wrote towards the right of this block. Whenever the variable 'loops' approaches 10 the system will halt.

This is recognized as a relative operator: it relates two values in literal terms. Tap on the blocks palette Operators group, after that, seek the other two diamond-shaped blocks upward as well as downward, one with the '=' sign. There are both contrasting operators: '<' contrasts two quantities and is activated once the left component is less than the right one, and '>' activates if the left value is greater versus the right value.

Tap on the block palette control tab, identify the 'if' block, and press and move it to the script field until lowering it simply below the say 2-sec block loops. The shift loops would naturally be surrounded by 1 row, therefore press and shift to transfer it so that it attaches to the lower part of your 'if' then row rather. Tap on the blocks palette Looks section, after this select and move a say Hello! Put it within your 'if' then block for 2 secs. Tap on the block palette Operators list, then press and move the n > n block inside the diamond-shape gap in the if-then block.

The if-then component is an implicit block, indicating that the blocks within it would only operate if a criterion is fulfilled. Press on the Blocks palette Data list, move and put the reporter loop block in the initial blank square in your n>n row, now press on the next blank square, and enter the '5' number. At last, press the term 'Hello!' in the say Hello! For a frame of 2 secs and enter 'That's high! '.

Press on flag green. The program will initially function as already with the cat sprite calculating from zero upwards. Whenever the figure hits 6, the very first number exceeding 5, the 'if' block will start to activate, and also the cat sprite will react to how big the figures get.

Big congrats: now, you can use variables and conditional expressions!

Self-Project: Response Timer for Astronauts

So it's time to create stuff a bit more immersive: a response timer constructed to respect British ESA astronaut Tim Peake as well as his time onboard the International Space Station.

If you'd like to preserve your current system, then unlock a fresh task by tapping on File and New. Enter a title by pressing on File and Save Project prior to when you start: Name it 'Astronaut Reaction Timer.'

This proposal is premised on two pictures-one as a stage backdrop, the other as a sprite-not inserted in the constructed-in funds of Scratch. Press on the raspberry logo to open the Raspbian list, shift the mouse cursor to the web, and then select Chromium Web Browser to install them. Enter rpf.io/astronaut-backdrop in the browser whenever the tab has opened, accompanied by the ENTER button. Right-tap on the space image and select the 'Save image' button, next pick the Downloads file, and press the Save key. Click the link in the search box, then insert the file and ENTER key.

Once more, right-tap on Tim Peake's image and select the 'Save image as...' button, then select Downloads file and press save button. Either you can exit Chromium or keep it open with those two pictures saved, and utilize the taskbar to turn over to Scratch 2.

User Interface

If you have read this book from the beginning, you must be acquainted with the user interface for Scratch 2. The current task directions will depend on you to recognize where items are; if you overlook where to search anything, at the start of this chapter, reflect at the user interface image for a reference.

Begin by right-pressing on the on-stage cat sprite and tapping Delete to erase it. Discover the control systems on the point at the lower left of the Scratch 2 display and select the symbol on the install backdrop. In the download file, locate the file Space-background.png, tap on it to pick it, after this select Ok. The context of the simple white stage will modify to the image of space, and the field of scripts will be substituted by the area of the background. You can catch over the background here but just tap on the Scripts marked section at the upper end of the Scratch 2 window as of now.

Attach your latest sprite to the top of their sprites panel by pressing the upload sprite button, adjacent to the terms 'New sprite:' in the download file, locate the document Astronaut-Tim.png, tap to pick it and select OK. The sprite displays instantly on the screen but may not be in the center: press it and move it with the cursor and put it, so it's close to the bottom third.

With your new history in position with your sprite, you're committed to introducing your software. Begin by constructing a new 'time' variable, ensuring that you pick 'For all sprites' before you press OK. To choose it, press on your sprite – either on the point or in the sprite panel – and after this, insert a block from the Events section to the script field when tapped. After that, just insert a say Hello! For 2 secs block of Looks section, then tap to alter it to say 'Hello! Tim Peake, British ESA astronaut, here. Are you prepared for this?

Insert a wait 1-sec block from the Control section; after that, a say Hello! block. Modify the block so that it says 'Hit Space! 'And then introduce the Sensing section refresh stopwatch block. This regulates a specific variable for measuring stuff developed into Scratch and can be used to moment how fast you can respond throughout the game.

Insert a wait until Control block, then move a principal space that has been pushed? Block sensing into its blank space. This may stop the software before you click the SPACE button onto the keyboard. However, the clock will proceed to operate – calculating precisely how long the notification informs you to 'Hit Space!' 'And you just press the SPACE key, basically.

Now you'll have to inform Tim how long it would take you to push the SPACE button, but in a manner that would be simple to read. To do just that, you will require a block of Operators join. This requires two quantities, like variables, and unites them one by one – recognized as conca10ation.

Begin with a say Hello! Block, then move and put the Operators' Enter block on the word 'Hello! '. Type 'Your reaction time' in the very first bar, remember to insert an empty space at the ending, then move the other join block inside the next bar. Move a clock reporting block to the center box from its Sensing section and enter 'seconds' into the final box – ensuring to have an empty space at the beginning.

Ultimately, move a fixed time to 0 Block data parameters towards the edge of your list, and then substitute the '0' with an announcing block for the timer. You're already prepared to check your game via pressing on the green flag just above the level. Be prepared, and you'll receive the text 'Hit Space!' if you could somehow defeat our best rating, click the SPACE button as fast as you can!

By measuring approximately how much the International Space Station has already moved in the period, it required you to click the SPACE button, centered on the reported velocity of seven kilometers every second of the station; you may expand this plan more. Initially, develop a new 'distance' parameter. Observe how the blocks within the Data section instinctively alter to demonstrate the fresh variable, and yet your system's current blocks of time-variable continue to stay the same.

Insert a fixed distance to 0 blocks and move a ● * ● Operators block over the '0' specifying multiplication. Move a block of recorded time onto the initial vacant space, and put the digit '7' into the second. Your joint block interprets distance to time once you're completed * 7. This will take a moment to push and multiply the SPACE button by seven to acquire the distance in kilometers journeyed by the ISS.

Insert 1 block of waiting 1 sec and alter it '4 secs.' Then, move and say Hello to the other! Block and link two combined blocks to the end of your chain, much like you did previously. Enter 'In that time, the ISS moves around' in the initial blank space, ensuring to provide the space in the end and enter 'kilometers' in the final white area, again recalling the space at the beginning.

Eventually, move a circular block of operators into the center empty space, and move a block of operating distance further into the fresh vacant space it produces. The round block culminates numbers down or up to their closest whole number, so you'll receive a simple-to-read whole number rather than an ultra-accurate but tough-to-read amount of kilometers.

To operate your software, press the green flag, then check how long the ISS moves in the duration it requires to reach the SPACE key. Consider starting to save your system once you've completed, so in the long term, you could even conveniently install it again without needing to initiate from the start!

Self-Project: Swimming in Sync

Many games are using more than one button, so this plan illustrates this by utilizing the buttons on the keyboard to provide two-button power.

This task can also be viewed online at rpf.io/synchro-swimming

Build and store a big venture like 'Synchronized Swimming.' Within the stage control category, tap on the Stage, and then tap on the Backdrops menu bar. Press from the palette on a water-like blue coloration, then select the color icon fill and click mostly on white background.

Right-click on the cat symbol and then tap on the 'delete' button. To view a collection of built-in sprites, press the 'choose sprite from library' button in the sprite field. Tap on the Animals section, after this 'Cat1 Flying', and then press OK. That sprite is indeed great for swimming initiatives.

Press on the fresh sprite, after which move two Events blocks further into scripts field when space code is activated. Tap the little downward arrow on the first block with the term 'space' and select 'left arrow' from the menu of probable choices. Move and put a Turn15 degree underneath the left arrow pushed block. After this, do alike with your second Events block, excluding select 'right arrow' from the menu.

To check your system, tap the upper or lower button. You can view the cat sprite copying as you do, corresponding to the path you select on the keypad. Acknowledge that this time you didn't have to press on the green flag; that's because the Events target blocks that you were using were also effective throughout all times, even though the system doesn't operate in the classic sense.

Follow the similar moves once again, except this time selecting 'down arrow' and 'up arrow' to activate blocks for the Events, and transfer 10 steps then move -10 steps for Movement blocks. Now click the arrow keys, then you'll see your cat could even move around and swim back and forth as well!

To create the movement of the cat sprite more naturalistic, you can alter the way it displays – recognized as its costume in Scratch language. Select the cat sprite and then press the Costumes icon just above the palette of blocks. Tap the 'cat1 flying-a' outfit and select the round X symbol in its upper right side to disable it.

Right-click on your freshly renamed 'right' outfit. To make a copy, tap 'duplicate.' To pick it, tap on the copy, press on the left-right turn over the icon, and change the name of it to 'left.' You'll end up having two 'costumes' for the character, that are accurate mirror pictures: one labeled 'right' with your cat looking right, and one labeled 'left' of your cat looking left.

Press on the Scripts section just above the costume section, then moves two change suits to just the left Looks blocks underneath the right arrow or left arrow Events blocks, moving one below the right arrow block to interpret the switch suit to just the right. Once more, press the arrow keys, the cat really seems to swim along its path.

However, we require more divers for synchronized swimming within the Olympic model, so we want a way to fix the location of the cat sprite. Insert a block of Events when pressed, and apply a go to x: 0 y: 0 Motion block underneath – alter the numbers if essential – as well as a point toward 90 Looks block. Then, tapping on the green flag will shift the cat to just the center of the stage and turn to the right.

Insert a repeat 6 block to generate further swimmers – modifying from the reset worth of '10' – and insert an established copy of myself Control block in there anyway. To make it happen that the swimmers don't swim in the identical path, insert a 60-degree turn block overhead the copy block but quite inside the 6-block repeat. Tap the green flag, and so now attempt the arrow keys to view the health of the swimmers!

You'll require some songs to finish the Olympic look. Press the Sounds window beyond the palette of blocks, and press the icon 'Pick New Sound from Library.' Tap on the Music Loops section, then press on the little play icons till you discover some songs you prefer - we've selected 'dance around.' Press the OK key on the keyboard to select the music, and afterward tap the Scripts menu to access the script area once more.

Apply another one to the script field if you press Events block, and then insert a forever Control block. Within this control block, insert a play audio dance until the block is finished – recall to search for the title of any type of music you pick – and tap the green flag to check your new system. Hit the red octagon to end the program as well as mute the audio if you'd like to end the tunes!

Ultimately, by introducing a new event button to your project, you can mimic a full choreographed dance. Insert Events block when space key has been pushed, then perhaps a swap costume to block right. Under that, bring a repeat 36-block – recognizing to modify the predefined value – inside it a move 10-degree block move as well as move 10-step.

To begin the system, tap the green flag and then push the SPACE button to attempt the fresh practice! Don't neglect to back up the file once you're done.

Self-Project: The Sport of Archery

Now you're actually becoming a real master at Scratch; it is indeed the moment to operate on something a bit more difficult: an archery game, in which the player will have to beat a target with just a bow and arrow swinging arbitrarily.

This task can also be seen online at
https://projects.raspberrypi.org/en/projects/archery

Begin by loading the Chrome internet browser and entering rpf.io/archery-resources with the ENTER key to be pressed. It only requires a couple of seconds for the game to install the functions. Turn back to Scratch 2, then tap on the file list and then Load Project. At the left side of the screen, tap on 'pi' in the Places panel, and after this, the 'Downloads' file, then select ArcheryResources.sb2 and then press Open. Whenever you decide to delete the material of your latest project, you will be questioned: if you've not stored your updates, press Cancel and thus save those, or else press Ok.

The task you've inserted includes background and a sprite, but nothing of the real game-making software: inserting that will be your responsibility. Begin by inserting a block when pressed, then perhaps a block of message1 displayed. At the edge of the line, press on the down arrow and after that 'New Message' and enter 'New Arrow' before pressing on the OK key. Your block then recognizes the latest arrow broadcast.

A broadcast is a signal from one portion of your system that any certain part of your system will get. To do something, insert a message1 block once you obtain it, and alter it once more when you receive a fresh arrow. You can simply tap on the down arrow this time then select 'new arrow' from the menu; you wouldn't have to build the text anymore.

After acquiring a new arrow block, insert a go to x: -150 y: -150 blocks and a fixed block size to 400 percent. Bear in mind that it isn't the standard values for all those blocks, so you'll have to adjust them when you move them to the script field. Select the green flag to determine what you've achieved up to this point: The arrow sprite used by the player to hit the obstacle will leap to the stage's lower part-left as well as triple in size.

Insert motion replicating shifting to offer the player a test as to when the bow is pulled, and the archer takes target. Move a forever block, accompanied by only a 1-sec glide to x: -150 y: -150 blocks. Change the initial white box that indicates '0.5' rather than '1,' then add a random selection -150 to 150 in both of the remaining two white packets. This implies that the arrow slides in an arbitrary path across the stage for a discrete location-creating it much tougher to strike the target!

Press once more on the green flag, and you'll notice what this block could do: the arrow sprite is now floating all around the field, reaching various portions of the goal. You don't have any way to lose the arrow at the goal just yet. Move a block into the script zone once the space button is clicked, accompanied by a stop all Control button. At the edge of the block, press the down arrow and move it to a place all leftover scripts in the sprite block file.

If you missed inserting the new blocks to your software, press the green flag to restart it, and after that , push the SPACE button: you'll notice the shifting arrow sprite. This is the beginning, but you have to keep it appear just like the arrow is going to the goal. To check your game once more, insert a repeat 50 block and then by a size alter by -10 block; now tap on the green flag. This time, your arrow seems to travel farther from you and onto the destination.

You have to insert a method of keeping the rating, to make the match enjoyable. Always in the identical block stack, insert an-if then block, ensuring it's beneath the 50 block repeat and not within it, with such an interacting color? Block detecting in its diamond-shaped difference. Press on the tinted box at the side of the Sensing block to pick the right color, after this tap on your enemy's yellow bull's-eye on the point.

Just so the player realizes they've achieved, insert a block play audio boost and a claim 200 points for such a block of 2 secs within the if-then block. Ultimately, introduce a new arrow block again to the lower part of the block pile to offer the player the next arrow every other time they shoot one, underneath as well as outside the if-then block. To begin your game, select the green flag and attempt to reach the yellow bull's eye: if you do so, you'll be honored by an audience cheer as well as a 200-point rating!

The game does function, but it's a bit difficult. Utilizing what you studied in this section, consider expanding it to include points to reach other goal sections than just the bull's-eye: 100 marks for red, 50 marks for blue, and so forth.

Chapter 5

Tips and Tricks for Python Programming in Raspberry Pi

Designed by Guido van Rossum, Python has got popularity from just a casual project released in 1991 to a mighty programming language supporting different types of projects now. The advantage of using Python is its test-based nature compared to Scratch, which has a visual environment. In Python, you write necessary instructions utilizing simplified language and a particular format. In this format and instructions, the computer makes the necessary processes.

Python is best for those professionals that have experience working with Scratch as it provides more flexibility and increased traditional programming conditions. Python is considered difficult to learn; however, with more practice and extra work, learning Python is very much possible. Anyone can do programming from easy calculations to very complex games.

Basics of the Thonny Python IDE

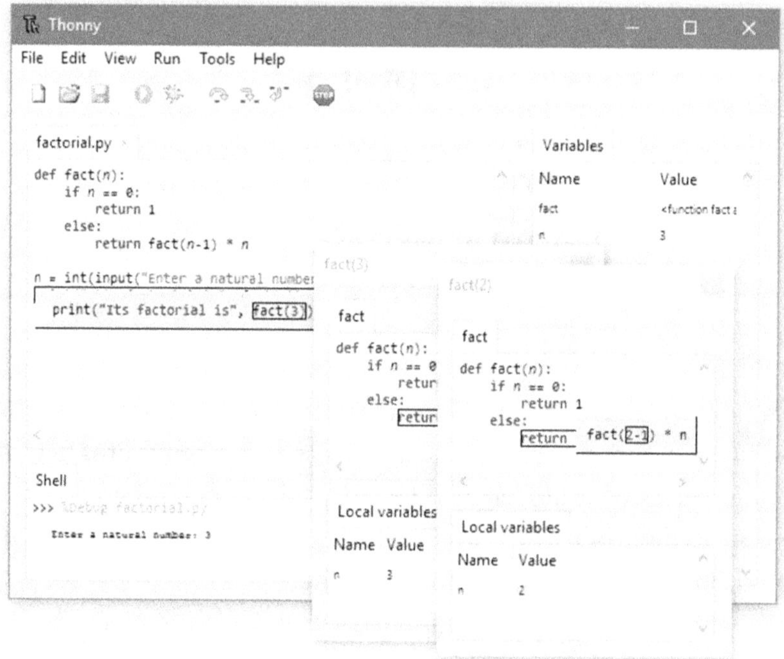

Figure 7: Thonny Python IDE

Toolbar

Thonny has a simple interface that contains friendly icons representing the menu. It allows you to create, load, save and use Python programs. One can also test it in different ways.

Area of Script

The script area plays a very important role as it helps in writing programs and divide into a more important area of your programming, and a little side margin to represent the line numbers.

Python Shell

Python plays a role in typing individual instructions. These instructions can run immediately after clicking the Enter key and give information related to programs that are running.

Variables Area

Any type of variable created by you in the program goes to variables area along with specified values for display purpose for the purpose of convenient references.

Creating your First Python Program

Similar to many others by default installed programs on your Raspberry program, Thonny can be accessed through the menu. For this purpose, click on the raspberry icon, go to the programming section, click on the Thonny. After a while, the user interface of the Thonny will appear.

Thonny is a complete package well-known as the IDE; it works to integrate all the required tools to write and develop software as a singular user interface. There are different types of IDE's available, some of these IDE's support a bunch of programming languages. On the other hand, Thonny supports only one language.

Contrary to Scratch, which provides you with building blocks that are visual in nature, for your program, Python is a rather traditional language of programming that requires everything to be writ10. If you want to start building your first program, click on the Python shell area given on the lower side of the Thonny window, and write below-given instructions before pressing the Enter key.

    print ("Hey, World!")

As you press the Enter, your program starts to run immediately. Python will provide the feedback in the shell area carrying the message Hey, World. The message with these wordings appears because the shell provides a direct link to the Python interpreter. Its sole work is to interpret your instructions. This mode is called the interactive mode, and it is just like a face to face conversation where you get the reply of what you say or write. However, it is better not to use Python in an interactive mode, go to the script area given at the left side of the Thonny window and then restart your programming again:

print ("Hey, World!")

As you push enter button this time, nothing special is happening, but a blank line appears in the script area. In order to make this program's version working, press the Run icon given in the Thonny toolbar. As soon as you do this, you will be requested to save your program, write a descriptive name, and click the save button. When your program is saved, two messages pop up in the shell area of Python.

">>> %Run Hey World.py" and

"Hey, World!"

Very first lines are some sort of instructions from Thonny carrying a message for the Python interpreter to start the recently saved program. The 2nd message is about the output of the program; it is the same message you ask Python to print. After this step, you are able to write and run your first ever Python program in interactive as well as script models.

Next Task: Loops and Code Indention

Python deploys a unique way of controlling the particular sequence where the programs are running; the sequence is called indentation. You can create a new program by just clicking on the New icon + given in the Thonny toolbar. This way, you will not lose already existing programs. Thonny will form a new tab on the top side of the script area. You can start after tying the following:

```
print("Start of Loop!")
```

```
for i in range (10):
```

The first line is for creating a line carrying a simple message similar to the Hey World program. The 2nd line will initiate a definite loop that functions very similar to Scratch. A counter named as i is specified to the loop. The symbol, colon (:) instruct the Python to include the next instruction in the loop. For smooth working, Python utilizes the indenting code approach. The very next line begins with four blank spaces, which Thonny includes when you pressed the key ENTER after the 2nd line.

```
print("Number Loop", i)
```

The blank spaces force this line towards the inside in comparison to the remaining lines. The function of the indentation is to guide Python to identify the difference between instructions given outside and inside of the loop. The code which is in10ded is then considered as being nested. As soon as your press the Enter towards the end of the third line, Thonny will in10d the automatically as it considers it a part of the loop. If you want to remove it press the Backspace key one time before going to 4th line:

```
print("Finish of Loop!")
```

With this step, your four-line program will come to an end. The first line stays outside the loop and runs only for one time. 2nd line is responsible for setting up the loop while the 3rd line remains inside the loop and also for just one time. On the other hand, 4th line, similar to the first line, sits out the loop.

```
print("Start of Loop!")
```

for i in range (15):

print("Number Loop", i)

print("Finish of Loop!")

Press the Run icon, do the program save step as Indentation, and check the shell area for its upcoming output.

Start of Loop!

Number Loop 0

Number Loop 1

Number Loop 2

Number Loop 3

Number Loop 4

Number Loop 5

Number Loop 6

Number Loop 7

Number Loop 8

Number Loop 9

Number Loop 10

Number Loop 11

Number Loop 12

Number Loop 13

Number Loop 14

Finish of Loop!

Indentation is one of the strong and important parts of Python and also responsible for the program to not run as was expected. As you check for issues in a program via the debugging process, make sure Indentation is not behind this. Python normally supports an infinite number of loops, which has no end to it. In order to replace your existing program to an infinite loop, make changes in line two to read:

while True:

If you press the Run icon this moment, an error will emerge: the name 'i' is not defined. This happens due to deleting the line which controls and give a value to the variable i. To correct it, just edit line 3, so it is not able to utilize the variable named:

print("Loop running!")

Press the Run icon, after doing so, a message with the wording 'Start of Loop!' will emerge followed a very long string of messages 'Loop running.' The message carrying 'Finish of Loop!' can't be printed as the loop has no end. Whenever Python completes printing the 'Loop running!' message, it automatically transfers to the starting point of the loop and starts printing it again.

To stop this, press the Stop icon given on the Thonny toolbar; this process is called interrupting the program. After doing this, a message will pop up in the Python's shell area,

After which the program will stop running.

Conditionals and Variables

All types of Variables do more function besides controlling loops in almost all types of programming languages. Let's initiate a new program by pressing the New icon visible on the Thonny menu. After doing so, write the below-given code into the script area:

```
userName = input ("Can you please tell your name?")
```

Press the Run icon, save and give Name Test to your program, and observe the changes happening in the shell area. First of all, you'll be requested for the name. Put your name in the given shell area, and press ENTER. As they are merely the instructions in the program, no special thing is going to happen. Only meaningful activity will happen in the variables area, which will show the variable as well as its value. The area of Variables will remain unaffected when the program isn't working. They make it convenient to check what is being done by your program.

If you want your program performs something better with the name, it is important to give a conditional statement through typing the following:

```
if userName == "Mary":

        print("Access granted!")

else:

        print("Access denied!")
```

It is important to note that when Thonny finds that your code required to be indented, it automatically does the same. The only problem is it doesn't understand when is the code is required to stop being indented. Therefore, you need to delete the given spaces yourself. Press the Run icon and put if required, your name in the shell area. After doing so, you are going to receive the message 'Access denied!'. Press option Run again and type the name 'Mary' carefully. By doing so, the program will recognize you as admin and will grant access.

The == symbols instruct the Python to perform a direct comparison, in10ded to check whether the variable userName is the same as in the text, also known as a string inside your program. If you are dealing with only numbers, you can perform other types of comparisons, for example: > check if a number is bigger than some other number in comparison, < is used to check if it is less than another number, while => is to check if the number is equal to or bigger than other numbers. Technically speaking, these symbols are called comparison operators.

Comparison operators are known to be used in loops. To do so, delete lines from 2 to 5, and type the following:

```
while userName != "Mary":

    print("You are not admin – access denied!")

    userName = input ("Please tell your name? ")

print("Access granted!")
```

Press the Run icon one more time. This time around, instead of quitting, the program asks for your name to confirm that really are the admin, just like asking for an easy password. To exit the loop, you can type 'Mary'; if it doesn't work, press the Stop icon given on the Thonny toolbar. This way, you have now learned to use both conditionals and comparison operators efficiently.

Self-Project: Turtle Snowflakes

By now, you learned how Python works. Now the time is right to learn about graphics and create some snowflakes. In essence, physical robots have shapes similar to their animal namesakes. For example, turtles are constructed to only move in a straight line, either lift or lower a pen. When we convert it to a digital version, it means to start or end, drawing a specific line with its movement.

Opposite to other languages, e.g., Logo along with its variants, Python doesn't have this turtle tool. However, it has numerous add-on codes to provide it a turtle power. These codes libraries have numerous codes that include new information and instructions to increase the capabilities of Python. These codes libraries are provided into your programs through an import command. Form a new program through pressing on the New icon, and writing the following:

```
import turtle
```

For using the instructions given in the library, use the library name, and then add a full stop and complete it with the instruction name. It feels hard to type your user name repeatedly, therefore, choose a smaller variable name. It can be as short as one letter, or you can use twice the pet name. Therefore, type the following:

```
var = turtle.Turtle()
```

To check the program if it is working or not, give the turtle a task to do. So type:

```
pat.forward(50)
```

Now press icon saying Run and save the program with the name Turtle Snowflakes. As soon as the program is saved, one new window with the name of Turtle Graphics will appear. This window will show the results of your program as your turtle, Pat, will go forward for 50 units forming one straight line.

After this step, go back to the main Thonny window. Possibly, it will be hidden on the backside of the Turtle Graphic window, so click the minimize option visible on the Turtle Graphics window. Another option to switch back to Thonny's main window is to press the Thonny entry present in the taskbar on the upper side of the screen. After this, press the Stop button in order to terminate the Turtle Graphic window.

Writing each and every movement instruction is a difficult task to do; therefore, delete line three and form a loop to perform a difficult task of creating shapes:

```
for i in range(1):

    pat.forward(50)

    pat.right(30)

    pat.forward(50)

    pat.right(60)
```

Now run the program, var will draw one parallelogram.

To convert it into a shape similar to the snowflake, press the Stop icon Thonny's main window and form a loop which circles your loop through adding the below-given line for line 3:

```
for i in range(5):
```

And the below-given line at the lower side of your program:

```
pat.right(18)
```

It is hard for your program to run it because the existing loop is not rightly indented. For fixing it, press at the beginning of each line of the current Start of Loop from line 4 till line 8 and push the SPACE key for up to 4 times to make indentation correct. After this step, your program will look like the following:

```
import turtle

        var = turtle.Turtle()

        for i in range(5):

        for i in range(1):

                pat.forward(50)

                pat.right(30)

                pat.forward(50)

                pat.right(60)

                pat.right(18)
```

Press icon saying Run, and see what happens in the turtle: It will form a parallelogram, similar to it has done before, but after completing this parallelogram, it will curve 18 degrees and form more parallelograms repeatedly, until it has drawn at least 10 parallelograms that are overlapping on the screen giving it a shape of a little snowflake.

When a robot draws the turtle on a big piece of paper, it is single-colored; on the other hand, Python's simulated turtle comes with a wide range of colors. Now include new line three and four, resulting in bringing the current lines down:

```
        turtle.Screen().bg color("red")
```

pat.color("blue")

Run the program once more; you can observe the impact of your new code. The background color shown on the Turtle Graphics window will turn red, while the snowflake color changed to blue.

If you want more colors, you can choose randomly from a list through a random library. For this purpose, go to the top of your current program and put the below-given wordings as line 2:

import random

Turn the background color through line 4, e.g., from red to yellow. After this form a fresh variable is known as 'colors' though putting a new line 5 given below:

colors = ["blue", "orange", "green", "red"]

This kind of variable is known as a list and is famous for square brackets marking. For our current case, the list contains all the possible colors in10ded for the snowflake parts; however, it is still necessary that you command the Python to select one new color for each repeating loop. At the finishing point of the program, write the following but keep in mind that it should be indented with up to four spaces it becomes the part of only the outer loop:

pat.color(random.choice(colors))

Now, press icon saying Run and the following words will be shown once more: snowflake-stroke-ninja-star. The only difference this time is that Python will select a random color on its own from the list you provided as it forms each petal one by one to give an attractive look to the snowflake.

To turn the snowflake to look similar to the actual snowflake and not like the ninja star, include an additional line 6, right below the colors list, and write the following:

```
pat.penup()

pat.forward(45)

pat.left(22)

pat.pendown()
```

Two instructions that are important to move a physical pen off and bring it on the paper are penup and pendown through a turtle robot. However, in the virtual world, just ask your turtle to finish sketching lines. This time, instead of utilizing a loop, you will create a function. It is a portion of code that is in your access all the time, similar to making your personal Python instructions.

Start the process by removing the code for sketching snowflakes based on the parallelogram; this means everything which is between and also includes the pat.color("blue") command starting from line 10 to pat.right(18) present in the line number 17.

Quit the pat.color(random.choice(colors)) command, and type a hash symbol (#) at the beginning of the line. This process means commenting out a command, and imply that Python will disregard it. To include different explanations in your code, adding comments will help you in this regard. These explanations help in understand the codes when you read them after some time has passed or given it to some other persons to use these codes.

Design your function named as 'branch,' simply through typing the below-given instructions in line 10, downward the pat.pendown():

```
def branch():
```

This code will explain your function, i.e., branch. As you click the
ENTER key, Thonny acts to put in indentation for commands of the
function. Write down the following, while paying keen observation
to indentation. This is important because somewhere you need nest
code as deep as up to three indentation levels.

```
for i in range(3):

for i in range(3):

pat.forward(15)

pat.backward(15)

pat.right(22)

pat.left(45)

pat.backward(15)

pat.left(22)

pat.right(45)

pat.forward(45)
```

At the end of the all, design a new loop towards the bottom side of
your program but still higher than the commented-out color line for
running, calling your newly formed function:

```
for i in range(8):

branch()

pat.left(22)
```

Press the Run key and see the graphics window because var sketches by acting on your instructions. Greetings! The snowflake prepared by you is now looking more like a snowflake.

Self-Project: RPG Maze

This project will take you to a complex and fully text-based game. This project much comprehensive and demands more creativity and intelligence. Now you will make a maze game by using Python. Obey the following instructions.

Go to the address rpf.io/rpg-code in any Web browser. Right-click on the page save the page. Press the Save button, then push the Load icon in Thonny. Search the file you downloaded and go to the Load button.

Now click icon saying Run. The game's output will in the shell area at the bottom of the Thonny window; press the maximize button so the window becomes large so you can read easily.

The game is very simple until now. There are only two empty rooms. The game starts from the Hall, and you can type 'go south' to go to the kitchen. You can now type 'go north' to go back to Hall. The player can also type 'go east' or 'go west,' but the game will error because there are no rooms on east and west.

But you can make the game more interesting by adding rooms to it. Add the Bed Room to the west to the Hall by finding rooms in a variable in the script area. You use a comma to expand it. Give the following instructions to the program:

        'Bed Room' : {

        'east' : 'Hall'}

The exit is not given, so you need to add an exit. After line ends, add a comma and provide the following instructions:

'west': 'Bed Room'

Now, if you are standing in the Bed Room, type 'go east' to enter the new room. Type 'go east' to return to the Bed Room while standing in the room.

If you want some more fun by adding an object to the room, you will need to change the room's dictionary. Find Bed Room dictionary present in scripts area, add a comma at the end of the line 'west' : 'Bed Room' and then press ENTER and give following instructions:

'item' : 'door key'

Now, if you run it again, you will see a new item 'door key' in the game. You can pick it up and can add it to your inventory.

Here you can make it more interesting by adding a devil to the kitchen, which should be avoided by the player. Just find the kitchen dictionary and add the 'devil' after adding a comma to the above line as you added the key above. Following is an instruction that is to be given for adding devil:

'item' : 'devil'

It is time to activate the devil, so it may be able to attack the player. Just scroll to vary button and type these instructions adding a comment with hash symbol helps you to remember this action:

if 'item' in rooms[currentRoom] and 'devil' in

rooms[currentRoom]['item']:

print('A devil caught you, and the game is now over!')

break

After this, run it again, but the devil added will not make much fun. You have to add more items to make it more interesting. You have to make a winnable if the player leaves the room by keeping the inventory items with him safely. Now you can add a Park. It very simple and the same as you added a room above in the program. An exit is to be added to the Bed Room dictionary. For this add following lines:

        'north' : 'Park'

Include a new room to the dictionary of main rooms but don't forget to add a comma above:

        'Park' : {'south' : 'Bed Room'}

Now further add a drink object to Bed Room dictionary, and also a comma, where necessary ,to the above line:

        'item' : 'drink'

Here you add a specific logic to check if the player has all the inventory items, tell them they have won the game. You can do so by following instructions:

        if current room == 'Park' and 'door key' in inventory and

            'drink' in inventory:

        print('You have won by escaping from the house')

After this, run the game and move to the Park while having the key and drink items with you. Never go to the kitchen room because there is a devil. You also have to add a few instructions for the sake of knowledge of players about how to complete the game. Add the following instructions at the top of the program where the function instructionsFunction() is present:

Reach the Park along with a drink and a door key by avoiding the devils.

Chapter 6

Physical Coding
using Python and Scratch

Coding is more important than performing front end stuff on the screen. You could also manage electrical equipment attached to the GPIO pins of your Pi using programming.

When people speak of 'programming' or 'coding,' they of10 think regarding software - and rightly so. However, coding can even be about much more than the operating system: it can significantly affect the world via hardware. This is termed physical computing.

Physical computing, as the title indicates, is very much about manipulating real-world stuff through your initiatives: hardware, not software. You are utilizing physical computing whenever you adjust the software to your washer, adjust the weather on your programmable heating system, or push a button at the traffic signals to cross the lane easily. Thanks to one major element, the Raspberry Pi is indeed a good product for studying regarding physical computing: the general-purpose input/output (GPIO) header.

Establishing the GPIO Header

Placed at the upper portion of the Raspberry Pi circuit panel and appearing like two lengthy rows of metallic pins, the GPIO header is to attach equipment such as light-emitting diodes (LEDs) and connectors to the Pi for command under the software you make. The term can seem somewhat complicated, but somehow it explains the part well. The pins can also be used for either input or output; they have really no defined function. They are recognized as headers whenever columns of pins are displayed on a circuit panel. Thus termed as general-purpose input/output header.

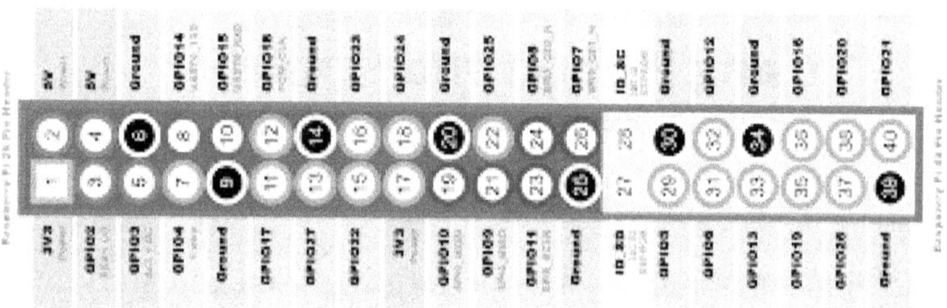

Figure 8: GPIO Header

The header of the Raspberry Pi GPIO is composed of 40 male pins. You can use some pins in your physical computing project activities, a few pins offer control, whereas other pins are restricted to interact with add-on equipment, such as the Sense HAT (see Chapter 7). There are many kinds of pins, and each has a specific role. Let us see the roles in the below table.

3V3	A forever-on 3.3V Power source, a certain voltage that is taken by Raspberry Pi to operate from within
5V	A fixed 5V Power source, the exact voltage as taken by Raspberry Pi at the micro USB controller level
GND	It is a ground connection that helps in completing the circuit for the power source

GPIO XX	They are the available pins for the programs starting from the number 2 and going till 27
ID EEPROM	These are the pins reserved to be used along with HAT (Hardware attached on top) as well as other similar accessories

Important note

The GPIO header from the Raspberry Pi is indeed a friendly and secure way to play with physical computing though it has to be handled carefully. Be aware not to flex the pins when attaching and detaching the equipment. Never attach two pins directly, unin10tionally or purposely, unless the guidelines of a task explicitly tell you to do it anyway: this is recognized as a short circuit, and may seriously harm the Pi, relying on the pins.

Tips and Tricks to Check the Electrical Parts

The GPIO header is just a portion of what you're going to need to start operating with physical computing; the other portion is composed of electronic components, the equipment you're going to manage from the header. Distinct systems are made in millions upon millions, but most GPIO developments are created using the mentioned common components.

A breadboard, also recognized as a solderless breadboard, could indeed significantly simplify the physical computing tasks. Instead of getting a handful of various pieces to be attached to wires, a breadboard allows you to plug elements and attach them via metal tracks stored underneath the exterior. Numerous breadboards also involve electrical distribution segments, which make your circuit's construction very simple and easy. To begin with physical computing, you wouldn't require a breadboard, yet this definitely helps.

Jumper wires, of10 recognized as jumper leads, link parts to the Raspberry Pi and with each other if you do not have a breadboard. These are present in three designs:

Male-to-female (M2F) that you will use to attach to the GPIO pins with a breadboard.

Female-to-female (F2F) that can be chosen to link different pieces together if you are not using a breadboard.

Male-to-male (M2M) that is required to make breadboard links from one component to another.

You might require all three kinds of jumper wire based on your task. If you are utilizing a breadboard, you can probably deal with only M2F and M2M jumper cables.

The sort of circuit you might use to handle a game system is a push-button switch, as well recognized as a momentary switch. Widely accessible having either two or four legs. Both of them will surely function with the Raspberry Pi. Also, the push button is a very important input device. You could even inform your system to observe for it to be pushed and then complete the work.

Another popular form of switch is a latching switch. While a push-button has only been activated when you keep it down, a latching switch-as you might see in a light switch-operates once when you turn it and remains active unless you turn it once again.

A Light Emitting Diode (LED) is used as an output device. You completely control it from your system. When it's on, an LED glows, and you'll notice them all across your home, varying from the tiny ones that let you realize when you've turned on your dishwasher, to the bigger ones that you could glow your rooms. LEDs come in a wide variety of forms, colors, and sizes, yet not all of them are appropriate for use with Raspberry Pi. Do not believe any claims made by someone that they are equipped for power supplies of 5 V or 12 V before checking it thoroughly.

Resistors are parts that regulate electrical current flow and are present in numerous measured values by using a unit named ohms (Ω). The greater the number of ohms, the greater the resistance a resistor can give. For physical computing tasks with Raspberry Pi, their greatest popular use is to secure LEDs from pulling too much voltage and harm themselves or the Pi. Although many electrical providers advertise handy bags comprising a variety of different widely used values to offer you enough versatility, you'll need resistors valued at around 330Ω.

Another output tool is a piezoelectric buzzer, commonly of10 called a buzzer or a sounder. However, when an LED generates light, a buzzer makes a sound – indeed, a buzzing sound. Within the plastic housing of the buzzer is a couple of metallic plates. These plates oscillate toward each other when productive to generate the buzzing noise. Two sorts of buzzers - exist active buzzers and passive buzzers. Please ensure you have an accurate buzzer as these are the easiest to use.

Other popular electronic equipment involves motors that require a special control board until they can be attached to the Pi, humidity and temperature detectors that can be expected to forecast the environment, infrared sensors that detect motion, and light-dependent resistors (LDRs) – input devices that sense light as a reverse LED.

Sellers worldwide offer the Raspberry Pi with parts for physical computing, either as separate pieces or in packages that give all you require to begin. A few of the trendiest retailers are:

- Adafruit

- PiSupply

- ModMyPi

- Pi Hut

- Pimoroni

- RS Components

To finish the task in this chapter, you should have no less than:

- Male-to-female (M2F) and female-to-female (F2F) jumper wires

- 3 LEDs of colors: Green, Red, and Yellow

- 1 active buzzer

- One breadboard and male-to-male (M2M) jumper wires (Optional)

- 2 Push-button switches

Color Codes for Resistor Measurements

Resistors are available in a wide variety of values, from null-resistance editions that are actually just part of cables to high-strength editions of the size of your leg. Some of these resistors have their amplitude values in digits on themselves. But they use a unique identifier displayed as colored stripes or bands across the resistor's body.

Color	1st/2nd Band	Multiplier	Tolerance
Black	0	$\times 10^0$	–
Brown	1	$\times 10^1$	±1%
Red	2	$\times 10^2$	±2%
Orange	3	$\times 10^3$	–
Yellow	4	$\times 10^4$	–
Green	5	$\times 10^5$	±0.5%
Blue	6	$\times 10^6$	±0.25%
Violet	7	$\times 10^7$	±0.1%
Grey	8	$\times 10^8$	±0.05%
White	9	$\times 10^9$	–
Gold	–	$\times 10^{-1}$	±5%
Silver	–	$\times 10^{-2}$	±10%
None	–	–	±20%

Figure 9: Color Code

Place it so that the community of bands is to the left, and also, the lone band is towards the right in order to access the actual value of the resistor. Try looking up its color in the table's '1st/2nd Band' section from the very first band to get the first and second numbers. This illustration contains two orange bands, all of which means '3' for a maximum of '33.'

Heading to the final clustered band - the third or fourth - check up the color in the row 'Multiplier.' This informs you which amount to multiply your original total by having the resistor's real value. There is a brown band in this case, which says 'x101.' That may sound complicated, but it's just scientific notation: '×10' literally says 'add a zero at the number's end.' If it was blue, for ×10 (power 6), it should mean 'add 6 zeroes after the number has ended'.

33, from the orange bands, especially with the added brown band zero, provide us 330 – that is the resistor value, analyzed in ohms. The ultimate band, on the right, is resistor sensitivity. That is plainly how near it is probable to be to its desired value. Affordable resistors may have a silver band, suggesting that they will be 10% higher or lower than their ranking, or no last band at all, suggesting that they may be 20% greater or lesser; the most costly resistors include a grey band, meaning that they may be below 0.05% of their rankings. Precision is not that critical for hobbyist initiatives: any sensitivity will typically work well.

If the resistor frequency exceeds 1000 ohms (1000 Ω), it is generally known as kilo-ohms (k Ω); if it exceeds a million ohms, it is mega ohms (MΩ). A resistor of 2200 Ω might be published as 2.2 k Ω; a resistor of 2200000 Ω would be defined as 2.2 M Ω.

Your First Software Program on Physical Computing: Greetings, LED!

Almost as publishing 'Hello, World' on the display is a wonderful first move in studying a language of programming, attempting to make an LED light up seems to be the conventional emergence to physical computing education. You will require an LED and 330 ohm (330 Ω) resistor for the given task, or as near to 330Ω as you can search, and furthermore female to female jumper wires (F2F).

Resistance is Essential

In the given circuit, the resistor is indeed a crucial element. It safeguards the Raspberry Pi as well as the LED by restricting the amount of voltage which the LED can attract. The LED could even pull much more current without it, and destroy itself – or the Pi – out. The resistor is recognized as a current-limiting resistor when utilized, such as this one. The greater the value, the dull the LED; the reduced the value, the more the LED glows. Never attach an LED to a Raspberry Pi without a current-limiting resistor, except if you are informed that the LED does have a suitable value designed-in resistor.

Begin by verifying whether your LED is working. Switch your Raspberry Pi so that the GPIO header is to the right side in two vertical lines. By using a female-to-female jumper wire to attach one end of your 330Ω resistor to the very first 3.3 V, then link the other side to your LED's long leg (positive or anode) with some other female-to-female jumper wire. Hold the last female-to-female jumper wire but also attach your LED's short leg-negative, or cathode-to the first ground pin.

The LED must glow, as long as your Raspberry Pi has been on. If not, double-check your device. Please ensure that you've not applied a resistor value too large, that almost all wires are properly connected, or that you've certainly chosen the correct GPIO pins to be the same as in the outline. Verify also the LED legs, since LEDs would only operate one way about; along with longer leg linked to the positive end of the circuit and also the shorter leg attached to just the negative.

After your LED is running, it is the moment to do its programming. Turn off the jumper wire from the 3.3 V pin then attach it to the GPIO 25 pin. The LED turns off, but no need to stress – it's common.

You are now capable of creating a program called Scratch or Python to switch the LED on as well as off.

Coding Skills

The tasks in this section require you to be satisfied by using the integrated development environment (IDE) of Scratch 2 and Thonny Python. If you haven't completed this already, shift to Chapter 4, Programming with Scratch, and Chapter 5, Programming with Python, and operate first via these initiatives.

LED Monitor in Scratch

Download Scratch 2 from the Raspbian menu, press more blocks in the palette of blocks, then select the 'Add an Ex10sion' button. Just press on the 'GPIO Pi' button, then select OK. This inserts the blocks from Scratch 2, which you require to regulate the Pi GPIO header. You'll recognize that the new blocks show up in the palette of blocks. They're accessible in the More Blocks section when you want to use them.

Begin by pulling a block onto the template files area when tapping Events, then put a set GPIO under it to extract a high block. You will have to select the pin number you are going to use. To access the drop-down list, press on the tiny arrow then press on '25' to inform Scratch that you are operating the GPIO 25 button.

To run your software, tap on the green flag. You'll notice your LED emit light; you've configured your initial task in physical computing! To end your software, press the red octagon; Observe how the LED remains lit? That's due to your software that has only informed the Pi to switch the LED on – that is what your set GPIO 25's 'output high' portion denotes for high block outputs.

Once more press on the green flag, but this time, your system switches off the LED. To make things more enthralling, add a control block forever, and a few wait 1 secs blocks to make a software that will turn the LED on and off per second.

Press the green flag and monitor your LED; it switches on for a second, switches off for a second, stays on for a second, and continues to follow the sequence until you press the red octagon to end it. See how that occurs when the octagon is tapped while the LED is still in it's on or off position.

Python LED Monitoring

Load Thonny from the raspberry list programming tab. Now press the new button to create a project and store it as a Hello LED. You should have an application named GPIO Zero to utilize the Python GPIO pins. You just require the section of the library to deal with LEDs for such a task. Upload only this library part by writing the following into the Python shell portion

```
from gpiozero import LED
```

You must then let GPIO Zero understand what GPIO pin the LED is linked to.

Class these as follows:

```
led = LED(25)
```

Next to each other, such two lines offer Python the authority to influence LEDs linked to the GPIO pins of the Raspberry Pi and inform that which pin-or pins-to handle if you really have much more than one LED in the loop. Run the following command to influence the LED:

```
led.on()
```

To disconnect the LED again, type:

```
led.off()
```

Awesome, you now have power over GPIO pins in Python from the Raspberry Pi! Attempt to retype those two commands. Whereas if LED is already turned off, led.off() will do nothing; the very same applies if the LED is on and you write led.on().

This software imports the LED feature mostly from the gpiozero library (GPIO Zero), as well as the time library, sleep feature, after which builds a limitless loop to switch the LED on for a moment, switch it off for a moment, and repeat. To view it in activity, press the run button: Your LED will start flashing.

To Utilize a Breadboard

If you consider utilizing a breadboard to house the parts and create the electrical systems, the upcoming tasks in this chapter will become much available to accomplish.

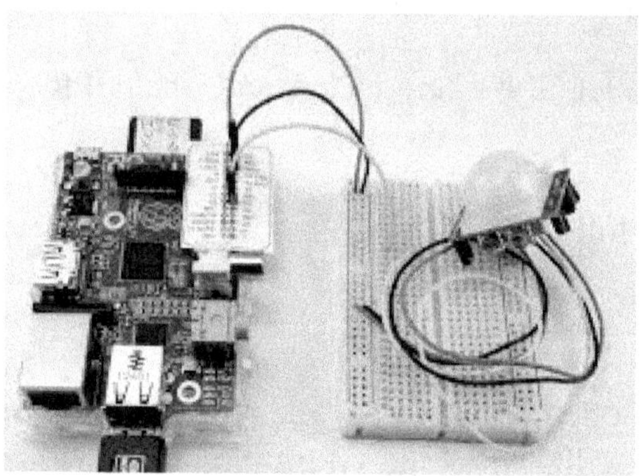

Figure 10: Breadboard

A breadboard is lined by gaps-spaced, 2.54 mm apart to suit elements. In these gaps are metallic strips that behave like the jumper wires that you have used till now. These ex10d across the board in columns, with many of these boards getting a gap down the center to divide these into two parts. Numerous breadboards have letters over the top and figures down the sides as well. These enable you to identify a suitable hole:

A1 seems to be the top-left corner, B1 seems to be the hole to the extreme right, while B2 is one hole back from there.

The disguised metallic strips attach A1 to B1, but no 1 hole will ever be linked to almost any 2 holes except if you insert a jumper cord to yourself.

Greater breadboards of10 have rows of gaps labeled with red and black or red and blue lines down the bottom. These are all the electricity rails, and thus are made to create cabling simpler: you can attach a separate wire from the ground pin of the Raspberry Pi to one of the supply rails – typically labeled with a blue or black stripe as well as a minus icon – to offer typical ground for several modules on the breadboard, if you're going to do the same if your loop requires 3.3 V or 5 V energy.

It's easy to connect electrical equipment to a breadboard. Simply match their leads (the sticky-out metallic pieces) up with either the holes and move them carefully till the element is mounted. You might use male-to-male (M2M) jumper wires for links you require to create outside those the breadboard creates for you. Use male-to-female (M2F) jumper wires for linkages again from the breadboard to just the Raspberry Pi.

Do not attempt to pack more than one lead element or jumper wire on the breadboard under one tiny hole. Make sure, apart from the separation in the center, the gaps are linked in columns so that a lead element in A1 is attached electrically to anything you introduce to B1, C1, D1, and E1.

Upcoming Moves: A Button to Read

Outputs such as LEDs are individual, but GPIO's input/output part indicates that you can utilize pins as inputs, as well. You'll require a breadboard, male to male (M2M), and male-to-female (M2F) jumper wires, as well as a push-button switch for this kind of task.

Begin with the push-button attached to your breadboard. If your push-button has just two legs, verify that they are in the breadboard's distinct numbered columns. If it contains four legs, switch it so that the ends from which the legs appear are along with the columns of the breadboard, and the flat leg-free ends are at the upper and lower side. Link your breadboard's ground rail to Raspberry Pi base pin; after this, attach one leg of your push-button to a male-to-male wire on the floor rail. Lastly, attach the other leg – the one on the identical end as the leg you recently linked while using a four-leg switch – to the Raspberry Pi's GPIO 2 pin to a male-to-female jumper cable.

Studying a Scratch Button

Begin a fresh Scratch system, and it moves a block into the script location when pressed. Attach a set GPIO to the large block output, and then choose the number 2 from either the drop-down to suit the pin you included in the push-button. To arrange the pin as an input, tap on the bottom arrow at the block end, then select 'input' from the menu.

Now, if you press on the green flag, nothing changes. That is true because you have informed Scratch to choose the pin as an input, but not exactly what to do about it. Push a block to the terminal of your pattern probably forever, after this slide an 'if' block within it. Is the GPIO great at spotting? Block, move it towards diamond-shaped space of the 'if' portion of the stack. Then use the drop-down to pick the number 2 to indicate the GPIO pin to test. Move a say hello, at last! Block into the other portion of the block for 2 secs and fix it to say 'Button Pushed! '. For now, ignore the 'if-then' portion of the block empty.

There's a lot of stuff going on over there but begin by checking it. Press the green flag and then press the breadboard button. Your sprite will inform you the button was pushed. You have interpreted an input from the GPIO pin correctly!

Maybe you've realized the 'if' GPIO 2 is high? Then the portion of the block is again empty. The software that keeps running whenever the tab is eventually pushed is in the other part of the block in the meantime. That would seem complicated, since pushing the button is sure to make it go high? In reality, it really is the inverse. The GPIO pins of the Raspberry Pi are usually high, or on, whenever configured as an input, and pressing the button pulls them back to the low.

Take a look again at your circuit: see just how you link the button to the GPIO 2 pin, which offers the positive portion of the circuit, as well as the ground pin. When the button is pressed, the current is pulled weak via the ground pin on the GPIO board, and the Scratch software stops running the code in your 'if' gpio 2 is high? Finally, block and execute code to the other portion of the block instead.

If all that feels puzzling, understand this: whenever the pin appears to be going low, a button on a Raspberry Pi GPIO pin is pressed, not when it will go high!

Push the LED as well as resistor back to circuit in order to expand the software even farther: recall to attach the resistor to the GPIO 25 pin as well as the long leg of the LED, and also the short leg of the LED to just the floor rail on the breadboard.

Lift the Say Button pushed! For 2 secs block the block toolbar from the script area to remove it, now start replacing this with a set GPIO 25 to higher block performance – consider changing the GPIO number by using the drop-down arrow. Insert a set GPIO 25 to production low block-make sure to alter the values to the presently unused if GPIO 2 is high? Then a piece of a block.

Tap on the green flag and then press the button. So as long as you grip the button down, the LED will turn on; let it go, and the LED will go dead again. Bravo: You are managing one GPIO pin dependent on another request.

Using a Python Button

To begin a fresh task, press the new button in Thonny, and the Save button to select it as the Input button. Applying a GPIO pin as a button input is quite comparable to just using the pin as an LED output, but you require to upload another portion of the GPIO Zero library. Type the script field below to:

```
from gpiozero import Button

button = Button(2)
```

GPIO Zero offers the **wait-_for_press** feature to have software operate when the key is pushed. Type these as follows:

```
button.wait_for_press()

print("It works perfectly")
```

Press the run button, and then click the push-button. Your text would then publish at the lower part of the Thonny window to the Python shell: you have published an input from its GPIO pin effectively! If you'd like to launch the software again, you will have to press the Run button once more. Since there is no circuit in the software, it will exit as quickly as the text has been published to the screen.

If you've not already completed so, insert the LED and resistor back into that same loop to broaden your system even farther. Know to link the resistor to the GPIO 25 pin as well as the long leg of the LED, and the short leg of the LED to the floor rail on the breadboard.

You will have to compile both the button as well as LED components from the GPIO Zero library to monitor an LED and to interpret a button. You'll need the Time library sleep feature as well.

Go straight to the top of your application, and enter the first two lines as mentioned below:

    from time import sleep

    from gpiozero import LED

Write **button = Button(2)**,below the line:

    ledvalue = LED(15)

Remove this line **print("It works perfectly")** and there write:

    ledvalue.on()

    sleep(2)

    ledvalue.off()

Your completed system must look like as follows:

    from gpiozero import Button

    from time import sleep

    from gpiozero import LED

    button = Button(2)

    ledvalue = LED(15)

    button.wait_for_press()

    ledvalue.on()

    sleep(2)

    ledvalue.off()

Press the Run button, then click the push-button switch. The LED should switch on for about three seconds and then switch off afterward, and the system will quit. Congrats, you can now handle the LED with an input button in Python.

Make Some Disturbance: Monitoring a Buzzer

LEDs are a wonderful machine for output, but do not use more if you search in another direction. The quick fix: buzzers that can detect sound anywhere in the house. You'll require a breadboard, male to female (M2F) jumper wires, and an effective buzzer for such a task.

If you don't use a breadboard, use female-to-female (F2F) jumper wires to attach the buzzer.

In aspects of circuitry and coding, an effective buzzer can indeed be treated the same way as that of an LED. Reiterate the loop you created for the LED. However, substitute the activated buzzer with the LED and take the resistor out, as the buzzer would require more input to operate. Use your breadboard as well as male-to-female jumper wires to attach one leg of the buzzer with the GPIO 15 pin, and another to the test board. Unless your buzzer contains three legs, ensure that the leg labeled with a minus symbol (-) is attached to the floor pin or that the leg marked 'S' or 'SIGNAL' is linked to GPIO 15, so attach the final leg - normally the center leg - to the 3.3 V pin.

Managing a Buzzer in Scratch

Reconstruct the very same software to make the LED flash or activate it if you stored it before developing the project button. To pick number 15, use the drop-down within the configured gpio to output high blocks so that Scratch manages the appropriate GPIO pin.

Tap on the green flag, and your buzzer will begin to bumble: a second on, as well as a second off. You should use a passive buzzer instead of an active buzzer if you can only lis10 to the buzzer clicking once every second. A passive buzzer requires a vibrating transmitter in which an active buzzer produces the constantly changing signal, identified as an oscillation, to create the metallic plates oscillate itself. Using Scratch, when you merely switch it on, the plates just swing once and then pause - creating the 'click' sound until your software turns the pin on or off another time.

To silence your buzzer, press the red octagon, but be certain to do this when it doesn't produce a sound, else the buzzer would continue to produce sound until you start your system again!

Managing a Buzzer in Python

Monitoring an active buzzer via the GPIO Zero library is nearly the same as handling an LED since it has on and off mode. However, you require yet another act: buzzer. Begin and save a fresh task in Thonny as Buzzer, then type like mentioned as follows:

```
from time import sleep

from gpiozero import Buzzer
```

Just like LEDs, to handle it, GPIO Zero will want to understand which pin your buzzer is attached to. Class these as follows:

```
buzzervalue = Buzzer(10)
```

Your software beyond that is nearly similar to the one you created to monitor the LED; the only distinction (other than a different GPIO pin number) is that you are using buzzer instead of led. Class these as follows:

```
while True:

buzzervalue.on()
```

```python
sleep(2)

while True:

    buzzervalue.on()

    sleep(2)

    buzzervalue.off()

    sleep(2)
```

Press the run button, and the buzzer would then start buzzing: a second on, and a second off. If you're running a passive buzzer instead of an active buzzer, you'll just notice a slight click per second rather than a constant buzz. This is due to a passive buzzer that requires an amplifier to produce the continuously shifting signal that causes the plates to vibrate within the buzzer.

To quit the system, press the Stop button, but ensure that the buzzer does not make a noise at the time, or it would proceed to beat until you operate the software again!

Scratch Operation: Traffic Lights

Already you remember how to operate buttons, buzzers, and LEDs as outputs and inputs, and you're able to create an illustration of real-world computing. Traffic lights, along with a button that you can push to pass the road. You will require a breadboard for such a task; a red, a yellow, and green LED; three 330 Ω resistors; a buzzer; a push-button turn; and a set of jumper wires from male to male (M2M) and male to female (M2F).

Begin by creating the circuit; attach the buzzer to the GPIO 15 pin, the red LED to the GPIO 25 pin, the yellow LED to GPIO 8 (GP8), the green LED to GPIO 7 (GP7) and the GPIO 2 (GP2) turn. Recall attaching the 330Ω resistors between both the GPIO pins as well as the long legs of the LEDs and attaching the second legs to the floor rail of your breadboard on all your items. Eventually, to accomplish the circuit, attach the floor rail to a ground pin (labeled GND), mostly on Raspberry Pi.

Develop ideas for a fresh Scratch 2 task, after which shove a block to the scripts area when pressed. You will then want to inform Scratch that the GPIO 2 pin is attached to the push-button to the handle in your loop, is a source instead of an output. Move the set gpio to the high block output via the more blocks toolbar tab underneath your block when selecting. Press on the bottom arrow next to '0' and from the drop-down menu choose number 2, then press on the bottom arrow just with the 'output high' and choose 'input.'

After that, you must generate your pattern of traffic lights. Push a block into your system everlastingly, and then line it with blocks to switch on and off the traffic signal LEDs in quite a pattern. Make sure that GPIO pins include which part connected: by using a red LED when utilizing pin 25, pin 8 the yellow LED, and pin 7 the green LED when in use.

Press on the green flag then monitor your LEDs. So first the red will illuminate, then the red and the black, after that the white, then the purple, and ultimately the red light will repeat the series again.

This sequence reflects which used by traffic signals in the UK. If you desire, you can modify the series to align sequences elsewhere.

To mimic a walker crossing, you require your system to see for pressing the button. To quit your system, press the red octagon if it is operating right now. Push an if-then block to your script area and link it with your traffic signal series in the 'if-then' segment immediately below your forever block. Consider leaving now the margin in diamond-shaped form unused.

A true passenger crossing doesn't really alter the brightness to red as soon as the button is pressed but rather gets ready in the pattern for the upcoming red light. Push a second to just the script area when you press on the block to construct that within your own system, accompanied by an everlasting block. Slide an if-then block and cover the diamond-shaped gap with a non-operator block accompanied by a gpio 2 is high? Block-make sure to alter the GPIO pin number by using the drop-down section. Lastly, build a fresh function named 'pushed' and put a set within the if-then block moved to 1 row.

This block stack observes for the pushed button and then sets the 'pushed' variable to 1. Holding a parameter this way allows you to save the knowledge that the button is pressed, regardless you might not operate on it immediately.

Return to the official block stack and then obtain the if block. Push an n = n Operator block into the empty if block, so push a moved investigator block into the vacant square first. Insert '0' into the empty square of second.

Select the green flag and display their series of traffic signals pass through. Select the push-button switch: it will seem like nothing has happened at first, but when the pattern has outreached its terminal– with only the yellow LED lit – the traffic LEDs will be off and remain off, all thanks to your creation 'pushed' variable.

All that is really remaining to do is certainly create your crosswalk button to do something else than switch off the lights. Search the other block in the main block stack then move a fixed gpio 25 into it to produce a high block-make sure to alter the standard GPIO pin number to suit the pin with which your red LED is attached.

Below that, already in the other block, build a template for the buzzer: move a 10-block duplicate, and cover it with fix gpio 15 to high output, hold 0.2 secs, reset gpio 15 to low output, and pause for 0.2 secs blocks, then adjusting the GPIO pin values to suit the buzzer part.

Lastly, add a fixed gpio 25 to output low block as well as a fixed pushed to 0 blocks below the base of your repeated 10 blocks and still in the other block – the last block that resets the parameter and saves the button, so that the buzzer series doesn't always loop permanently.

Press the green flag, and then press your breadboard to swap. After the pattern comes to an end, you will view the red light going on as well as the buzzer noise going on to let the road walkers understand that it's safe to walk. The buzzer prevents after a few seconds, and also the traffic signal series begins again and keeps going till you push a button another time.

Huge congrats: you have also coded your own entirely operational set of traffic lights, accomplish with crosswalk!

Python Operation: The Rapid Response Game

Since you remember how to utilize buttons and LEDs as outputs and inputs, you are capable of creating an illustration of true-world computing. A fast-reaction two-player game, built to determine who has the quickest response speeds! A breadboard, an LED and a 330Ω resistor, two push-button adapters, a few male-to-female (M2F) jumper wires, and some male-to-male (M2M) jumper wires are required for this task.

Begin by constructing the circuit: attach the very first switch on the left side of the breadboard to the 14-pin GPIO, the second switch on the right side of the breadboard to the 15-pin GPIO, the lengthier leg of the LED to the $330\,\Omega$ resistor that links to the Raspberry Pi GPIO 4 pin, as well as the second leg to the floor rail on all the parts. Lastly, attach the floor rail to the test board at Raspberry Pi.

Begin a fresh task in Thonny, and store it as a response Game. You will be using the GPIO Zero library LED but also button operations, as well as the time library sleep feature. However, instead of transferring the two GPIO Zero operations on two distinct segments, you can end up saving time and transfer to divide them next to each other, utilizing a comma symbol (,). Type the script area mentioned below:

```
from time import sleep

from gpiozero import LED, Button
```

Again, you'll have to inform GPIO Zero that which pins are attached to the two buttons as well as the LED. Type these as follows:

```
ledvalue = LED(5)

button_right = Button(20)

button_left = Button(19)
```

Now insert commands for turning the LED off and on, so that you can confirm that it is operating correctly:

```
ledvalue.on()

sleep(4)

ledvalue.off()
```

Press the Run button: for four seconds, the LED will switch on, and after that will switch off, and the system will leave. However, making the LED go off after precisely 4 seconds every time, for the objective of a response game is a little easy to predict. Add additional time import sleep line underneath:

from random import uniform

As its title indicates, the random library allows you to produce random numbers (with even a homogenous distribution here - see rpf.io/uniform). Search the sleep line (4) and transform it to read:

```
sleep(uniform(4, 10))
```

Tap on the Run button once more: this time, your LED will remain illuminated around 4 and 10 for such a random number of moments. Check to determine how of10 it requires for the LED to go out, after this press several more times on the Run button: you'll notice the time for every run is dissimilar, helping the program to be less predictable.

You'll have to insert a feature to transform the buttons into triggers for

Every player. Move to the quite lowest of the system and type:

```
def pressed(button):

print(str(button.pin.number) + " is the winner of the game")
```

Keep in mind that Python utilizes incision to find out which lines seem to be component of your feature; Thonny can instantly smudge the second line. After this, insert the following two sections to trace the gamers pushing the buttons-ensure that they should not be indented, or else Python would then consider them as a component of your feature.

```
button_right.when_pressed = pressed

button_left.when_pressed = pressed
```

Operate your system and attempt pushing one of its two buttons this immediately as the LED passes out. You can view a text at the lower part of the Thonny window for the very first button to be printed onto the Python casing. Unsurprisingly, every time any button is pressed, you'll also receive notifications – and they're using the pin number instead of a good label for the button.

To solve that, begin by requesting the identities of the gamers. Run the following command below the line from irregular uniform transfer:

```
name_left = input("Name of left player : ")

name_right = input("Name of right player : ")
```

Return to your system and replace the segment
print(str(button.pin.number) + " is the winner of the game ") by:

```
if button.pin.number == 19:

print (name_left + " is the winner of the game ")

else:

print(name_right + " is the winner of the game ")
```

Press the Run button, and enter both players' identities into the shell field of Python. Once you push the button this moment, recalling doing that as soon as feasible just after LED will go out, you would see that the identity of the gamer is printed rather than the number of the pins.

You will have to insert a new feature mostly from sys – short for system – library: quit to fix the issue of all of the other button taps being observed as finally winning. Type the command against the last Import line:

```
from os import _exit
```

Next, type the following at the conclusion of your feature, underneath the line print(name_right + " **is the winner of the game**") :

    _exit(0)

In this case, the incision is essential: _exit(0) must be enclosed into four spaces, queuing up with another: two lines at its upward and if two lines just above. This teaching informs Python to stop the game after pushing the first button, indicating the gamer for which, the second button is pushed won't get any bonus for losing!

Tap the run button, type the names of the players, stop for the LED to turn off, and also the winning player's name will appear. You can also notice two lines through Python on its own: the very first, **Backend terminated (returncode: 0)**, Python informs you that now it got your **_exit(0)** order and left the system; the other, **Resetting ...**, alerts you that the state of the system is being fixed. That's why you'll find the collection of variables there in the Thonny window vanish from the variables field.

Huge congrats: you have now created your very own physical game!

Chapter 7

Sense Hat Physical Computing

The Raspberry Pi contains a built-in technology to run a very useful type of add-on board known as HAT, also called the Hardware Attached on Top. HATs have the ability to support different types of equipment, including microphones, lights, and electronic relays, as well as screens to the Pi. Sense HAT plays a crucial role in the Astro Pi space mission. It is a collective project of the Raspberry Pi Foundation, UK, and EU Space Agencies. After reaching the orbit, astronauts using the Sense HATs, also known as Ed and Izzy. It is being used to not only run the code but also to perform the scientific experiments with the contribution of schoolchildren.

Though Ed and Izzy are in access for you to work on them by yourself, the similar Sense HAT hardware is available at all Raspberry Pi retailers. If you don't want to buy one by yourself, it is possible to simulate it in software.

Introducing the Sense HAT

The Sense HAT is a very important addition to the Raspberry Pi software. The Sense HAT contains an 8 by 8 matrix with up to 64 red, green, and blue programmable LEDs that are helpful in creating millions of colors. It has a five-way joystick controller along with sensors for smooth working.

Gyroscope Sensor

It is used to trace changes happening in the angle over time, through monitoring the direction of the gravity field of the earth. Technically the change is called angular velocity, a force that attracts things to the center of this planet. In simple words, the gyroscopic sensor can guide you when you move the Sense HAT with respect to the surface of the Earth and how fast it is rotating.

Accelerometer

It has almost the same function as the gyroscope sensor, but instead of monitoring an angle with respect to the Earth's gravity, it calculates the acceleration force in various directions. Using the collective data from both the sensors can help you trace where a Sense HAT is leading to what is the mechanism of its movement.

Magnetometer

It helps in measuring the strength of the magnetic field. This sensor is also very useful in monitoring the Sense HAT's movements through calculating the strength of the natural magnetic field of the earth. This way, a magnetometer can find out the north direction of the magnetic field. These three sensors are placed over one chip on the HAT's circuit board with the name 'ACCEL/GYRO/MAG'

Humidity Sensor

Its task is to measures the ratio of water vapor in the air, also called the relative humidity. The range of relative humidity varies from 0% at minimum to 100%, when the air is full of water vapor. Humidity data plays an important role in forecasting the rain.

Barometric Pressure Sensor

A Barometric or barometer plays a crucial role in measuring air pressure. Besides being used in weather forecasting, the barometer can track the movement, whether you are moving up or climbing down a mountain because the air is thinner on the height compared to the sea level.

Temperature Sensor

The temperature sensor, as the name depicts, measures the temperature of the environment. However, the reading can vary if the Sense HAT is hotter or colder than normal. There is no separate temperature sensor in Sense HAT, as it uses temperature sensors fitted on humidity or pressure sensors.

Installing the Sense HAT

After purchasing the physical Sense HAT, unpack it and count all the required pieces, i.e., the Sense HAT, four pillars or spacers, up to eight screws, and a few pins in a strip. Remove the strip pin until you hear a crack to get these pins. The function of spacers is to prevent the Sense HAT from bending. It will secure your Sense HAT and GPIO header from any damage.

Now, install these spacers by bringing the screws up from the lower side of the Raspberry Pi and putting these spacers onto the screws, line them up properly, and screw the last four screws well in the mounting holes. In order to check if all went well, Plug the power into the Raspberry Pi and LEDs of the Sense HAT illuminate in a rainbow pattern. You can switch it off again as the Sense HAT is installed now. To remove Sense HAT, remove the top screws, lift the HAT off, and take off the spacers from the Pi.

Hello, Sense HAT!

Similar to other programming projects, Sense HAT starts with a welcome message on its LED display. In the case of Sense HAT emulator, load it through clicking on the Raspbian menu icon, selecting the Programming category, and then pressing on Sense HAT Emulator.

Greetings from Scratch

To load Scratch 2 using the Raspbian menu, press the More Blocks options and then on the 'Add an Ex10sion' button. Press the' Pi Sense HAT' ex10sion and finally press the OK button. Now, the blocks to control features of the Sense HAT will open. Begin with dragging Events block to the script area, after it drags the scroll message block below this. Make changes in the text, so it becomes a 'scroll message Hey, World!

Now click the green flag present in the stage area and see your Sense HAT, a message will emerge slowly on the Sense HAT's LED matrix, and form each letter in turn; this shows, your program was a success.

After this, look at some other features of the scroll message block. You can change the rotation of the message as it is shown on the Sense HAT. Press the down arrow near 0 and alter it to 90; this time, the scroll message block show: Hey, World! with a rotation of 90. To bringing the rotation back to 0, press on the arrow next to 'in color white' to check a list of different colors to select from. Let's select the yellow color, press the green flag to confirm the change.

In the end, press the down arrow presents next to 'background off' to open a list of colors again. This time, the change in color will affect the LEDs that don't make the message portion of the screen. Choose any of the colors, let's say blue from these colors, and press the green flag. This time the message is bright yellow and looks attractive on a blue background.

Greetings from Python

Open the Thonny, through the Raspbian menu icon, selecting Programming, and pressing on any of the Thonny links. To utilize the Sense HAT in a Python program, it is necessary to import a library of the Sense HAT. Write the below-given code in the script area:

sense = SenseHat()

The Sense HAT library takes a message, do formatting to show it on the LED display. For this, type the below-given code:

sense.show_message("Hey World")

After saving the program with the name Hey Sense HAT, and click the Run button. Your message will slowly emerge on the Sense HAT's LED matrix. This is the indication that your program is a success.

There are more tricks in the show_message() function.

The parameters text_color=() and back_color=() are here to select the colors of the writing as well as the background, respectively. Instead of putting the names of colors, you have to specify the color as a trio of numbers. In these three numbers, the first represents red color in10sity; the second number shows the green in10sity in color, while the third number contains the in10sity of blue.

If you like to have names according to your choice, instead of RGB (red, green, and blue) values, you'll need to produce the variables.

This way, you the variable names to increase the reliability and readability of the code. Now, to be able to scroll complete messages, you can show individual letters. Delete the sense.show_message() line, and put the below-given wordings in its place:

sense.show_letter("A")

When you press the Run button, the letter 'A' appears on the Sense HAT's display, which shows your program was successful.

Next Steps: Drawing with Light

The Sense HAT's LED display can do more than just messages; e.g., it can be used to display pictures. Every single LED can be taken as a single pixel in the image of your choice. This way, it becomes easy to decorate your program with images and animation.

To produce drawings, you are required to change individual LEDs. There are up to eight LEDs in all rows of the display, and also in each column.

Pictures in Scratch

Create a new project in Scratch, saving the current project, and open the Sense HAT ex10sion through visiting the More Blocks category. After this, bring a 'when clicked' events block towards the script area, bring the set all pixels to white block below this area.

Now, press the green flag: you'll observe that all LEDs become bright white, and looking straight on these bright LEDs while running the program isn't a wise decision.

To turn off the LEDs, click the arrow present near the 'white' and pick another color, and run your program once again. All the LEDs will be turn off this way. If you want to change the current color, bring all the pixels to the off-script area to remove them, then change it with a set of pixels to the block R 255 G 255 B 255.

Now try other color values to get your favorite one. To get a picture, you are required to control individual pixels. To make your version of the LED matrix sample with up to two selected LEDs glowing in red and blue, replace your 'set all pixels' to R 0 G 255 B 0 block to make all pixels to R 0 G 0 B 0, bring up to two 'set pixel 0, 0 to white' blocks on the bottom side of it.

Press the green flag to check your LEDs light up similar to the matrix image. Greetings, you have learned to control individual LEDs.

Sensing the World around You

The Sense HAT's LED matrix provides you the fun along with the facility to take different readings from temperature to acceleration. Different sensors that measure humidity, pressure, and temperature work with the help of Sense HAT.

Environmental Sensing in Scratch

Open a new program in Scratch and save the older if you want. Use the More Blocks category to add an ex10sion. Now drag when clicked events block on the script area, and drag set all pixels to white block under it. Now set to set all pixels to off by using down arrow. Again drag say Hello for 2 secs Look block underneath the existing block. Find and drag pressure block from More Blocks category to get reading of pressure sensor. You have to drag right over Hello! in you say Hello for 2 secs block.

Click the when clicked, and you will get current pressure reading by Scratch cat from a pressure sensor in millibars.

Now, if you have to switch to the humidity sensor, just replace the pressure block with humidity block. Simply run the program, and the reading of the current humidity of surroundings will be displayed.

It is also very simple to switch to a temperature reading. Just replace the humidity block with the temperature block and run the program again. This time you will get the temperature in degree Celsius. Due to heat generated by Raspberry Pi, the temperature may not be exact.

Inertial Sensing

The inertial measurement unit is a combination of a gyroscopic sensor, accelerometer, and magnetometer. There are multiple sensors in IMU which take readings from surrounding indecently, and some sensors give a combined reading.

It is important to understand how things can move around 3 axes before you move forward towards IMU. The Sense HAT and Raspberry Pi are attached. They can move side-to-side on x-axes, back and forward on y-axes, and up and down z-axes. They are also able to rotate around these axes. The rotation around the x-axis is called 'roll'; around y-axis 'pitch' and around z-axis 'yaw.' Rotating the Sense HAT along its short axis is called 'pitch.' Rotating along its x-axis is known as 'roll,' and spinning on the table is called 'yaw.'

Inertial Sensing in Scratch

Open a new program in Scratch and load Sense HAT ex10sions. Now drag a when clicked Events block on the script area drag a set all pixels to white under the upper block. Now turn it into set all pixels to off block by using the down arrow. The next step is to drag a forever block and fill it with say Hello! This is to be placed below the existing blocks. Now add join block along with corresponding blocks of pitch, roll, and yaw to get readings of IMU. It is necessary to add space and commas to make readings more legible.

It's time to run the program by moving the Sense HAT and Raspberry Pi, but you have to be careful. Because of the readings of pitch, roll and yaw changes as you tilt the Sense HAT.

Inertial sensing in Python:

Load a new program and save it as a Sense HAT Movement in Thonny. Use the following lines to start the program. Remember to use sense_emu if you are using Sense HAT emulator:

sense = SenseHat()

sense.clear()

Observe the readings split along three axes. Sense HAT can also provide the measurement of movement. But for this purpose, it is to work in a loop.

The Sense HAT is taking the reading of three axes; X or left and right; back and forth; and Z or up and down. These readings are difficult to read because variables are not containing the whole numbers in reading.

Joystick Control Scratch

Load a new program in Scratch and load the load Sense HAT ex10sion. Drag a when clicked block, and a set all pixels to white block and turn it to black by using the down arrow. The joystick works equivalent to cursor keys and ENTER key on the keyboard.

Drag a when space key pressed block on the script area and convert it into when up arrow key pressed by using the arrow. Drag a say Hello! for 2 secs block.

Pushing the joystick up, the Scratch cat says, "Hello". Change the say Hello! for 2 secs block as say Joystick Up! for 2 secs. Add something for each of the five ways of the joystick that can be pressed. Now you can press the joystick in various directions to see you your messages appearing through the Scratch cat.

Finally, you can move the joystick and watch that LEDs glow in different colors. You can also turn them off by pushing the joystick-like push-button.

Chapter 8

Raspberry Pi Camera System

Linking a Raspberry Pi Camera System to your Pi allows you to get hold of high-resolution pictures, film video clips, and develop creative projects for the computer's field of vision.

If at any point, you've planned to design things that can visualize – regarded as computer's field of vision in the field of technology – then the additional Raspberry Pi camera system is a pretty good place to begin. The Camera Module, a tiny square circuit panel with a slender ribbon cord, attach to the Raspberry Pi Camera Serial Interface (CSI) connector and delivers high-resolution motionless pictures and shifting video impulses that can be made use of as it is or by being incorporated into your projects.

Kinds of Cameras

The Raspberry Pi Camera System is at one's disposal in two versions: the standard one and the 'NoIR' version. The dissimilarity is easy to determine: the standard version includes a green circuit panel, whereas the NoIR version contains a black circuit panel. If you desire to keep taking normal images and video clips in bright environments, the standard version must be used for the finest picture resolution. The NoIR version is termed as such because it does not have an infrared, or IR, exhaust, and it is designed to be used with channels of infrared light to capture images and video clips in absolutely dark environments. If you're constructing a nest container, surveillance camera, or some other night perception project, you need NoIR version-but remember buying an infrared source of light along with it.

The existing version of the Raspberry Pi Camera System, recognized as the 'v2' or 'Version 2.1' model, is built on a high-quality Sony IMX219 image detector – this sensor is identical to the one you encounter on the backside of your mobile and tablet. It is an 8-megapixel detector, which indicates that images can be taken with as much as 8 million pixels. It accomplishes this by taking pictures up to 3280 pixels broad by 2464 high: multiplying these two numbers results in a maximum of 8 million independent pixels!

The Camera System is able to capture motionless images as well as record video recording at Full HD quality - the same quality as several TVs - at an amount of 30 frames per second (30 fps). Through decreasing the quality, the camera can be adjusted to record at a higher frame frequency with quicker transition or by generating a slow movement effect: 60fps for 720p video recording and up to 90fps for 480p - or 'VGA' quality - recording.

Installing the Camera Module

Like any hardware add-on, the Camera Module should only be connected to or disconnected from the Raspberry Pi when the power is off and the power cable unplugged. If your Raspberry Pi is on, choose Shutdown from the raspberry menu, wait for it to power off, and unplug it.

Disassemble your camera package. You will discover a plain ribbon wire and a tiny circuit panel that is the camera package, actually. The ribbon wire has already been attached to the camera package throughout many situations; if not, flip the package upturned so that the camera lens goes on the lower part and search for a plain plastic linker. Thoroughly hang your fingernails across the corners of the stick-out and drag them out till the linker moves out partially. Drift the ribbon wire along with the silver corners downstream and the blue plastic pointing upwards, underneath the fold you already forced out, and move the fold softly back into position with a tap; no matter which edge of the wire you are using. When the wire is correctly mounted, it would be straight, and whenever you give it a soft pull, it would not drop out; otherwise, take the fold-out and attempt once more.

In a relatively similar way, mount the other edge of the wire. Recognize the connector on the Raspberry Pi Camera (or CSI) and draw out the fold softly upwards. When your Pi is placed inside a case, it may be simpler to uninstall the Pi. With the Pi situated in such a way that the HDMI port faces you, drift the ribbon wire in so that the silver corners come on your left side, and the blue plastic comes on your right side, then simply press the fold back. When the wire is correctly mounted, it would be straight, but when you grant it a soft pull, it will not drop out; otherwise, take the fold-out and attempt once again.

The camera package includes a tiny segment of blue plastic that covers the lens to shield it throughout production, delivery, and activation from damages. Discover the little plastic fold and softly take it off the lens so that your camera becomes fully prepared to be used.

Adjusting the Camera's Focus

A tiny plastic wheel normally comes with the Raspberry Pi Camera Package. It is in10ded for lens focus change. Although the factory-set focus is normally flawless, you could further drift the wheel across the lens and softly curl it to individually alter the focus when you are making use of your camera for an extremely close-up project.

Link the electric supply straight to the Pi, and allow Raspbian to be loaded. You will have to notify the Pi that it has one attached before you are able to make use of the camera: tap the raspberry symbol to activate the menu, select the Preferences section, and tap Raspberry Pi setup. Once the tool is successfully prepared, tap on the Interfaces section, locate the Camera element within the list, and tap on the circular radio button at the left side of 'Activated' to enable it. Tap Yes, and then the device prompts you to restart the Pi. Do it , and your camera will be prepared for use.

Running Tests on the Camera Module

You can make use of the raspistill gadget to verify that your Camera Module is fitted correctly and that you have allowed the Raspberry Pi Setup Tool interface. This is engineered to record pictures through the camera by making use of the Raspberry Pi Command-Line Interface (CLI), together with raspivid for video clips.

You will not be able to locate raspistill on the menu, unlike the programs that you have made use of until now. Alternatively, tap on the raspberry symbol to launch the menu, pick the section Accessories, and press Terminal. A black screen opens with green and blue text in it: this is the terminal that further enables you to gain access to the command-line interface.

To check the camera, run the following command into Terminal:

raspistill -o test.jpg

When you press, ENTER, you will see a big image of whatever the camera views on-screen. This is known as the live demo and continues for 5 seconds except if you notify raspistill differently. The camera can take a singular still image after this time runs out and stores it in your home directory with the title test.jpg. Enter the same order once again if you decide to grab another one – just remember to alter the title of the resulting file after the -o, or store it across the top of your previous image.

In case the live stream is inverted, you should notify the raspistill of the camera is repositioned. The Camera Module is built to get the ribbon wire falling from the lower edge. If it comes from the edges or the top, just like certain third-party camera mounting attachments, you can make use of the -rot option to turn the picture by 90, 180, or 270 degrees.

Employ the mentioned command for a camera placed with the wire falling from above:

raspistill -rot 180 -o test.jpg

In case the ribbon wire comes from the right side, make use of a 90-degree rotational worth; if it comes from the left side, use 270 degrees. In case your initial capture had been at an incorrect angle, attempt another to rectify it by making use of the -rot option.

Launch the File Manager from the Accessories section of the raspberry dropdown menu to view your picture: the picture you have collected, named test.jpg, would be in your household/pi directory. Locate it in the file catalog, and double-click it in a picture viewer to activate it. You can indeed fas10 the image to e-mails, post it online through the mobile app to sites, or move it to an additional storage gadget.

Presenting Picamera

Python, through the use of the handy picamera library, is by far the most adaptable method to manage the Camera Module. This provides you complete influence across the preview, image and video clip capture capabilities of the Camera Module, and enables you to incorporate them within your own programs – also merging with programs that make use of the GPIO subsystem via the GPIO Zero library.

Python Programming

The works in this section carry on familiarity regarding the programming language of Python, Thonny IDE, and the GPIO keys of the Raspberry Pi. In case you have not completed that, kindly work across the works in Chapter 5, Programming with Python, and Chapter 6, Physical computing with Scratch and Python.

In case the Terminal is open, shut it by tapping on the top-right X of the screen, then mount Thonny from the programming section of the raspberry menu. Store your latest plan as Camera, then begin importing your program's library functions by inputting the given in the script zone:

camera = PiCamera()

It enables you to use the camera feature to monitor the Camera Module.

To begin with, enter the following:

camera.start_preview()

sleep(5)

camera.stop_preview()

Select Run, and your display will fade away. You will see a complete screen demo of everything the camera can view. Attempt to push it about, or wave your hand across the lens front, and you will be able to see the adjustment that suits the image on the frame. Following 5 seconds, the demo will shut down, and your program will complete - but no image will be stored afterward as it does in the demo from raspistill.

If your demo is a false way upwards, you can spin the photo to see it back up the correct way.

Right below the **row camera = PiCamera()**, add:

camera.rotation = 180

In case the demo is inverted, that row will make things seem correct again. Just like with raspistill, camera. Rotation allows you to spin the picture by 90, 180, or 270 degrees, dependent on whether the wire comes from the Camera Module's right, upper, or left side. Remember to make use of camera.rotation at the beginning of every program you type, to prevent photographing the photos or videos in the incorrect way!

Now you are able to begin filming your animation with stop-motion! Place the camera device so you can view the items you're trying to trigger, and ensure it doesn't shift – if the camera shifts, the effect is ruined. Position the items in their initial locations, and press Run to start the system. In the recap, verify everything appears great, and then tap the push-button to obtain your first piece.

Slightly shift the items– the fewer you switch them among frames, the better the final animation will then be – so click the push-button to grab another image once more. Continue to do this before your animation is over: the further frames you catch, the lengthier your animation will then be.

When you're done, push CTRL+C to exit your software, and double-click on the screen animation file to view the images you've taken. To open the folder, click twice on any image and view it more specifically!

Yet all you own at present is a file filled up with unmoving photographs. You have to transform these into a clip to make an animation. Tap the raspberry icon to open the list, select Accessories, and select Terminal to do so. This introduces a command-line interface that enables you to write instructions into the Pi. Whenever the Terminal opens, shift to the file you created by entering:

cd Desktop/animation

It's essential that the 'D' of 'Desktop' is in the upper case; Raspbian is basically what is recognized as case-sensitive, meaning if you won't enter an instruction or file title the way it was actually writt10 it would not operate!

It requires software called avconv to capture and transform motionless photos in the file into a clip named animation.h264. Depends entirely on how much stills you've taken, this cycle will require a couple of minutes; once you notice the Terminal request reappear, you will realize it's over.

Locate the animation.h264 database in your animation file to watch the clip, and click twice to access it. Conversely, you can replay this from the terminal.

When the clip is loaded, you can view your animation with stop-motion coming to exis10ce. Bravo: You changed your Raspberry Pi into more of a po10t studio for animation!

Alter the -r 10 portion of the avconv instruction to a greater or lower amount if your animation moves very fast or quite slowly. This really is the screen resolution, or even how many motionless pictures there are now in a second of the clip. A smaller amount will allow the animation to operate slower yet appear less smooth; a greater number appears better; however, the animation will operate faster.

If you wish to save the clip, be certain to move and put it from your computer to your video clips file, or else, you will end up reversing the document the next moment you operate your system!

More Advanced Camera Configurations

If you'd like more authority over the Raspberry Pi Camera device, you could even select multiple settings by utilizing the Python pi camera database. These configurations are described below, alongside their standard values, to be included in your own projects.

1. camera.brightness = 70

That determines the camera photo illumination, from both the lowest at 0 to the fullest at 100.

2. camera.awb_mode = 'auto'

This configures the camera's instant white adjustment mode, and thus can be adjusted to any of the mentioned modes: auto, off, sunshine, cloudy, shadow, fluorescent, tungs10, spotlight, as well as horizon. If you figure that your images and video clips appear a bit yellow or blue, and then select another mode.

3. camera.contrast = 0

That establishes the contrast enhancement. A larger proportion will build stuff that looks quite in10se and strong; a lower proportion will make stuff appear more faded. You can choose any amount, for minimal comparison from -100 as well as 100 for maximum comparison.

4. camera.color_effects = None

This affects the camera's color combination presently being used. This configuration should ordinarily be left all behind, but if you offer a couple of figures, you can change the manner a camera records shade: attempt to develop a white and black picture.

5. camera.exposure_compensation = 0

This determines the camera's exposed control, so you can automatically monitor how much illumination is shot for every picture. It does actively monitor the camera function, unlike adjusting the screen brightness. For quite a gloomy picture, legitimate values vary from -25 to 25 for a really vibrant photograph.

6. camera.crop = (0.0, 0.0, 1.0, 1.0)

This helps you to trim the picture, cut sections off the edges and tops to get only the fraction of the picture you require. The figures mean X coordinate, Y coordinate, height, as well as width, and the full picture is obtained via default. Seek to which the final two numbers- a good first step is 0.5 and 0.5-and observe what impact such an environment has.

7. camera.shutter_speed = 0

This influences the speed at which the aperture can open or close while taking photographs and videos. Within microseconds, you may adjust the shutter frequency individually, including longer shutter rates functioning best in darker light, or quicker shutter rates in strong light. It should also generally stay in its standard, automatic configuration.

8. camera.framerate = 30

This specifies the number of photographs shot, or the screen resolution, to develop a video clip every second. A greater screen rate generates a quicker video, but more data storage occupies. Higher screen rates involve the use of a low rate that can be adjusted through camera.resolution.

9. camera.ISO = 0

That affects the camera's ISO level, influencing how responsive it is to illumination. Based on the light accessible, the camera adapts it instantly by reset. Using any one of the mentioned values, you could perhaps establish the ISO yourself: 100, 200, 320, 400, 500, 640, or 800. The greater the ISO, the best the camera operates in low-light surroundings, but the blurrier it shoots the photo or video.

10. camera.exposure_mode = 'auto'

This establishes the visibility mode, or indeed the reasoning used by the camera device to determine how to highlight a photograph. Off, night, auto, spotlight, backlight, seaside, snow, sports, very lengthy, antishake, fixedfps, and firecrackers are all feasible modes.

11. camera.hflip = False

This, when assigned to true, spins the camera picture beyond the horizontal plane, or X.

12. camera.resolution = (1920, 1080)

It determines the quality of the image or video being taken, portrayed by two figures for height and width. Lesser resolutions can use less memory space and enable a greater screen rate to be used; greater resolutions are also of greater standard but fill up more memory space.

13. camera.image_effect = 'none'

That refers to the clip stream, that will be apparent in the display and also the saved photos and videos, one of a series of camera results. Probable outcomes are fade, animation, contrast adjustment, color swap, color print, deinterlace1, deinterlace2, emboss, denoise, movie, hatch, zero, g pen, negative, enamel paints, contrast, pasteurize, pastel, drawing, decolorization, solarize, plus watercolor.

14. camera.meter_mode = 'average'

This governs how well the camera determines how much lighting will be accessible when determining its in10sity. The standard combines the in10sity of daylight present in the entire image; backlit, matrix, and spot are several other available modes.

15. camera.sharpness = 0

This handles picture clarity. Probable values range between -100 and 100.

16. camera.saturation = 0

It monitors picture brightness or even how vivid the colors are. Probable values differ between -100 and 100.

17. camera.video_stabilization = False

This switches on video stability once adjusted to Real. To minimize the shakiness of the recorded footage, you just want this unless the camera module shifts when you are filming, like if it is connected to a machine or is getting carried.

18. camera.rotation = 0

This regulates picture rotation, around 0 degrees to 90, 180, as well as 270 degrees.

19. camera.vflip = False

This, when adjusted to Real, turns the camera photo all across the horizontal, or Y, plane.

More relevant data on certain configurations and also additional configurations that are not publicized here can be observed at picamera.readthedocs.io.

It's not very nice to have to reboot your system anytime you take an image for your animation, so you have to modify it to operate in a cycle. However, except for the prior loops you've developed, it really requires a way to shut it elegantly. Or else, if you halt the system even if the camera preview shows, you won't be allowed to view the screen any longer! You have to utilize two specific commands to do it: **try and except.**

Begin by removing all after **camera.start _preview()**, after this enter:

frame = 1

This produces a fresh, frame variable that can be utilized by your system to store the existing frame figure. Soon, you'll utilize this to make sure you save a fresh file each time; without this, each time you push the button, you'll only be saving from over the upper edge of your initial photo!

After this, organize by entering your loop:

while True:

    try:

The latest attempt command informs Python to operate whichever code is within-which will be the photo capture function. Enter:

button.wait_for_press()

camera.capture('/home/pi/Desktop/animation/frame%04 d.jpg' %

frame) frame += 1

Those three sections of code contain a few smart tricks. The first one is in the title of the capture folder: applying %, 04d informs Python to select a figure and insert as many zeroes to the front as four-digit numbers are needed. Thereby "1" will change to "0001," "2" can change to "0002," as well as "10" can change to "0010." This is what you require in your system to maintain your documents in the proper sequence and also ensure you don't end up writing on a document you've only just stored.

At the conclusion of that step, the % frame informs Python to applying the dynamic frame figure in the file title. To ensure that every file is specific, the very last line - frame += 1 - increases the dynamic frame by 1. The frame will indeed be boosted from 1 to 2, the very first moment you push the button; the second time, from 2 to 3; and so forth.

Yet, at the point, when you are done capturing images, your code normally can't quite smoothly. You require an except for your try to form this possible. Recall erasing one incision amount on the initial line so that Python realizes that it's not a portion of the try segment.

Attempt to tap Run, but rather than pushing the keys, on the keypad, push the CTRL and C buttons. You don't have to push both keys simultaneously. Merely simply hit CTRL, push and leave C, and then leave CTRL. Such two keys are serving like an interruption, informing Python to avoid what it does. Without the exception of the KeyboardInterrupt: line, Python might instantly cease disrupting your display and end up leaving the camera teaser.

So, this was all about the Raspberry Pi Camera System. We hope you enjoyed reading it.

Conclusion

Anyone can use Raspberry Pi to build amazing projects like retro games, robots, their own operating system, etc. This book will help you to understand all these details step by step. You can easily control a computer with the help of Raspberry Pi; set up your own things by connecting circuits and wires directly to GPIO pins present on the board. You will also understand how to practice coding in Python and Scratch within the operating system.

I hope you found everything about the tips and tricks to learn Raspberry Pi programming in this book. Always remember that it takes time to master Raspberry Pi, and overnight results can't be expected until you practice it. Therefore, learn every detail in a phased manner, as explained in this book, and build your expertise.

References

https://www.raspberrypi.org/